TEACHING ABOUT
THE WARS

Jody Sokolower, Editor

A RETHINKING SCHOOLS COLLECTION

Teaching About the Wars is an updated and expanded version of an earlier Rethinking Schools publication, *Whose Wars? Teaching About the Iraq War and the War on Terror.*

Editor: Jody Sokolower

Design and Production: M.J. Karp

Special thanks to Sheilah's Fund of Tides Foundation, the teacher/writers, the editorial board of Rethinking Schools, and Harold Berlak.

A Rethinking Schools Publication

Rethinking Schools, Ltd., is a nonprofit educational publisher of books, booklets, and a quarterly magazine on school reform, with a focus on issues of equity and social justice. To request additional copies of this book or a catalog of other publications, or to subscribe to *Rethinking Schools* magazine, contact:

Rethinking Schools
1001 East Keefe Avenue
Milwaukee, Wisconsin 53212
800-669-4192
www.rethinkingschools.org

ISBN: 978-1-937730-47-5

TABLE OF CONTENTS

CHAPTER 1

Introduction

Breaking the Silence on War

Today in classrooms, as in the streets, there is too much silence

JODY SOKOLOWER

This collection of articles is a call to action. As the invasions of Afghanistan and Iraq have morphed into endless war in the Middle East, we believe there is an urgent need to bring serious study and discussion of the issues into the classroom.

J.D. KING

When the World Trade Center was attacked, the international crisis reverberated in schools all over the United States. In kindergarten through high school classrooms, teachers struggled to figure out age-appropriate ways to talk about the violence. Then, in that endless month leading up to the U.S. invasion of Afghanistan and during the contentious months before the U.S. invasion of Iraq, the worldwide debate about the war was echoed in classrooms. Teachers searched for curriculum as students expressed fears for relatives in the military and worried about the possibility of a renewed draft. A month before the invasion of Iraq, the *New York Times* declared that global antiwar protests were "a new power in the streets." After the invasion, at first there were demonstrations every day in major cities, then every month, then once a year. There was a flurry of political activity as the first high school alumni were killed, as military recruiters swarmed onto high school campuses.

Today in classrooms, as in the streets, there is too much silence.

Rethinking Schools first published a collection of articles on teaching about the Iraq War in 2005. Inspired by teachers' many requests for materials, it was titled *Whose Wars? Teaching About the Iraq War and the War on Terrorism.* As the time approached to revise and reprint, we were in a quandary. We kept hoping that the wars would be over; that Bush would be defeated and U.S. foreign policy would move in a less bellicose direction. Instead, under Obama, the war in Iraq continues, the war in Afghanistan has expanded, there is a growing U.S. incursion into Pakistan, and the United States continues to bankroll and defend Israel's war against the Palestinians. We could delay no longer.

> **WE NEED TO CREATE THE SPACE FOR STUDENTS TO SHARE THEIR OWN EXPERIENCE OF AND QUESTIONS ABOUT THE WARS.**

We know that it has become even more difficult to bring U.S. military strategy into the classroom. These wars are rarely on the front page or the nightly news. For most students, they are just a fact of life; for children in elementary school and middle school, the United States has always been at war. As attacks on teachers, teachers' unions, and tenure escalate, the job risk of venturing into controversial territory can seem too great. And it takes thought and sensitivity to effectively raise questions when many students have relatives who are fighting or who have been injured or killed.

It has never been easy to integrate "current events" into the curriculum. In many high school history classes, the current world doesn't show up until the last few weeks of the year, if it makes it at all. In elementary and middle schools, social studies has been squeezed out of classrooms by the NCLB-fostered obsession with testing. Figuring out how to have your class read a whole book or sneaking in a field trip are enormous feats. In this context, teaching kids about the ever-expanding landscape of war from Africa through Asia seems too much to ask.

So the silence in classrooms about the wars isn't surprising. But what does that silence tell our kids?

In 1992, just as the first U.S. war against Iraq ended and the embargo that would result in the death of a half million Iraqi children began, the feminist philosopher Susan Griffin published *A Chorus of Stones*. In this remarkable book, she explores the relationship between conspiracies of silence in families about incest or alcoholism and conspiracies of silence in countries about what happens in the name of war—her examples include the German extermination of Jews and the Allied bombing of Dresden. Griffin says:

> The troubling nature of censorship is clearer when it falls on the very young. A certain kind of silence, that which comes from holding back the truth, is abusive in itself to a child. The soul has a natural movement toward knowledge, so that not to know can be to despair.

Silence in our classrooms about the war is heavy with potential meaning:

▪ War is endless and inescapable, part of the wallpaper of life.

▪ The Middle East conflict is another one of those depressing subjects that is too complicated to understand, too impossible to change, and leading us toward an inevitable Armageddon.

▪ War under Bush was a legitimate subject for debate and critique, but Obama symbolizes hope—after all, he won the Nobel Peace Prize. To question Obama is to embrace hopelessness.

▪ Who are we to question, when textbooks bury our ongoing wars in a few comforting paragraphs? McDougal-Littell's *Modern World History* titles its brief section on the Iraq War "The Struggle Continues" and offers this summary: "Despite the coalition victory, much work remained in Iraq. With the help of U.S. officials, Iraqis began rebuilding their nation."

We have to break this silence, no matter what the pressure of tests or workload. The conflicts expanding out from the Middle East are among the most significant events happening the world. They are creating the history of tomorrow.

As the U.S. military's demand for soldiers expands, our high schools and middle schools have turned into recruiting grounds. There are more than 3,200 junior ROTC units in our children's schools, with about half a million students taking part. As the economic situation deteriorates, the racial and class discrimination of the poverty draft becomes more acute, for many of our young people feel they have no alternative to military enlistment. Recruiters flood our schools and stalk the malls. The Army, Navy, Marine Corps, and Air Force exceeded their recruitment goals for the 2009 fiscal year, sending 169,000 active duty recruits to training. As high school and even middle school teachers, we have a responsibility to support our students in analyzing recruitment documents and thinking critically about the short- and long-term effects of military service.

Central to popular education—social justice education—is connecting personal experience to knowledge to collective action. This means we need to create the space for students to share their own experience of and questions about the wars, particularly when those students have family members who have died, been injured, or are serving in Iraq and Afghanistan.

This collection is offered in that spirit. The articles and activities are drawn from our work over the past decade. There are areas that need updating and others that are incomplete (there is a particular need for more materials on Palestine and Pakistan). We hope that you will find useful materials and be inspired to adapt, update, and create new curriculum. When you do, please send it to us. In that way, you will be adding to an ongoing source for teachers committed to providing diverse sources of information to compare with the textbook and mainstream media version of the wars, as well as seriously studying the history and current strategies of antiwar activism, with a particular focus on the role that young people have played.

We want to empower our students and encourage them to act on their beliefs. We envision breaking the silences in our classrooms as part of an international effort to save our youth (all our youth—here in the United States, in the Middle East, all over the world) from war and more war. ▪

LUBA LUKOVA

Teaching in a Time of War

RETHINKING SCHOOLS EDITORIAL (Summer 2003)

Teaching during a war magnifies a dilemma for educators: how to deal with controversial matters in the classroom. In recent years, educators at all levels have grappled with this issue, and we at Rethinking Schools have received considerable feedback—both positive and negative—on the "Teaching About the War" emphasis in our quarterly publication and on our website: www.rethinkingschools.org.

Among our critics, some feel that schools should focus on the traditional curriculum and ignore world events. Others argue that controversial issues may be studied in the classroom so long as instruction is "balanced," and the teacher remains "neutral." Still others have suggested that certain Rethinking Schools editors should immediately quit teaching and move to Iraq or France.

DECIDING IN ADVANCE THAT EVERY ISSUE HAS TWO SIDES TO "BALANCE" IS AT BEST FORMULAIC, AT WORST PROPAGANDISTIC.

Although the call for a "balanced" curriculum is seductive, it is not a helpful way to frame our responsibilities as educators. "Balance" is a term that conjures images of fairness, equality, and justice. But it incorrectly suggests a two-

silence = complicity

sided inquiry: "We need to expose our students to both sides of the issue," we recently heard one school principal say.

But which two sides are those? Reducing social conflicts to just two sides and insisting that our task is to evenhandedly balance these two sides may be one route to avoid controversy, but it should not be our aim. Education is about making explanations—asking why things happen—and exploring alternatives, not about finding and then balancing two sides to an issue. Deciding in advance that every issue has two sides to "balance" is at best formulaic, at worst propagandistic.

For example, an investigation into the war in Iraq should begin with lots of questions. Teachers might ask: Who has supported this war and why? Who has opposed it and why? Historically, what has motivated U.S. policy toward Iraq? Are the stated reasons for the war—to halt the production of weapons of mass destruction, to liberate oppressed people from a brutal dictatorship, etc.—pursued by U.S. policymakers with equal vigor throughout the world?

Does United States conduct match these supposed objectives? Who benefited from this war? Who suffered? What is the significance of oil in this conflict? How have different media "constructed" the war for the U.S. public?

A critical inquiry such as this does not fit neatly into the "both sides of the story" model. In short, our aim should be creating a pedagogy of questions that strives to promote a deep understanding of the world, not some abstract idea of "balance."

It's not surprising that the demand for our curriculum to be "balanced" resurfaces at moments when the dominant or traditional story is under attack. When social movements challenge bias, inequality, or war, school officials (and these days, right-wing radio talk show hosts) begin the balance mantra. It's often an attempt to silence criticism. By contrast, when is the last time someone in a position of authority demanded that military recruiters on campus be "balanced" by the presence of War Resisters League activists or that the Pledge of Allegiance be "balanced" by critical discussions of the pledge's imperial and anti-immigrant origins in the late 19th century?

POLITICAL DECISIONS

The call for balance during the second Gulf War reflects a broader conservative vision that education should be neutral. But as historian Howard Zinn once wrote, "In a world where justice is maldistributed there is no such thing as a neutral or representative recapitulation of the facts."

Every curriculum begins from certain assumptions about the world, even if these may not be conscious. And, teachers make countless political decisions every day. For example, when a teacher puts up a Thanksgiving bulletin board instead of one that truthfully examines Columbus' encounter with the Taínos, he or she is making a political choice.

Virtually everything we do in our classrooms takes some kind of stance about the nature of our society. During a war that has caused thousands of deaths and serious injuries, massive property destruction, looting, and potentially frightful environmental consequences, it's impossible for our teaching not to comment—if only implicitly—on these events. If bombs—made in the United States, and paid for by the United States—are tearing into communities half a world away, inevitably our teaching will encourage students to accept or question these policies and actions.

But acknowledging this inherently political nature of curriculum doesn't mean that teaching is simply propaganda. We need to present students with a variety of positions, not merely those we personally agree with. And we need to encourage them to question all viewpoints, including our own. The best way to develop critical understanding of social problems is through direct engagement with diverse ideas. Finally, it is absolutely essential that students feel free to express opinions on controversial issues without fear of teacher reprisal or student condemnation.

Does this mean that teachers should avoid sharing their personal viewpoints? We don't think so. Teachers who take pride in never revealing their opinions to students model moral apathy. How teachers react to the burning issues of the day is itself a part of the curriculum. And to be silent in the face of global injustice teaches profound, and harmful, lessons. Nonetheless, teachers need to be alert to the ways that their behaviors can stifle questioning or dissent in their own classrooms. And teachers also must read their own political environments to assess how much freedom they have to teach honestly and responsibly.

The kind of inquiry that we propose is not neutral, but neither is it biased. Teaching is biased when it ignores multiple perspectives and does not allow interrogation of its own assumptions and propositions. A social justice approach, on the other hand, invites diversity of opinion but does not lose sight of important aims of the curriculum: to encourage deep questioning, to alert students to global injustice, to seek explanations, and to nurture activism. This is the kind of teaching we work toward. ▪

Learning from the Past, Talking About the Present

A 4th-grade teacher reflects on her own schooling and poses hard questions to her students about war

KELLEY DAWSON SALAS

I was a high school senior in Dearborn, Mich., during the Gulf War in 1991. We did not talk about the war at school. I remember feeling confused about why the war was happening, but I don't remember learning what was behind it. I remember my classmates making comments like, "We have to get the Arabs" (this in a school district that is now predominantly Arab American), but I don't remember anyone intervening to explain what was wrong with the hate and xenophobia in those comments.

Now the United States is in a second war in Iraq, and I am a 4th-grade teacher trying to help my students examine world events and the role the United States plays in them.

> **SOME PRINCIPALS CREATE A SCHOOL CULTURE THAT CONVINCES TEACHERS THAT WAR AND OTHER "POLITICAL" ISSUES ARE TABOO IN THE CLASSROOM.**

Some people think teachers should not teach about such controversial issues like war. Some principals instruct teachers not to teach about the war, and others create a school culture that convinces teachers that war and other "political" issues are taboo in the classroom. As the United States was gearing up to attack Iraq, I decided to ask my students what they thought about bringing discussions of the war into our classroom.

As part of our morning routine we share news from the children's lives as well as local and world news. In addition to our morning discussion time, we had spent several social studies lessons studying the crisis in Iraq, discussing what factors led to the current conflict, and listening to diverse perspectives on the impending war from people around the world.

One morning I shared a new piece of local news with students. At the request of a group of high school students, Milwaukee Public Schools Board Director Jennifer Morales had introduced a resolution requiring all intermediate and high schools in our district to dedicate at least one class period and one after-school event to studying the Iraq crisis. The resolution specified that age-appropriate materials be used and that diverse perspectives on the issue be explored in classrooms.

I asked my students whether they thought it was good for kids to study the war in school. In order to bring out a variety of opinions on the issue, I asked: "What are some reasons why students should learn about the war in school? What are some reasons why students should not learn about the war in school?" We made a T-chart and listed their responses.

One reason students shared for not learning about the war in school was that it would scare kids. We discussed this a bit and the students disagreed on what age was "old enough" to learn about the war and not feel scared. Several students said 5 or 6 years old was too young, and one said that it was scary for her even at age 9. One student commented that kids should not learn about or even think about war because they would become too focused on violence and would want to make war when they grew up. Another student suggested that families could inform their own children about the war.

Equally interesting reasons emerged for why students thought they should learn about the war in school. One student raised the idea that students and families need to know about the war in order to prepare for an attack on their homes or school. At least two students mentioned a lack of information at home: One student said that not all kids get newspapers or watch TV news, and another said that not all parents talk with their children about the war. One student suggested that if students learn about the war, they might be able to learn how to stop the war or how to avoid wars in the future. Another student said that kids need to have a chance to talk about the fears and worries that they have about the war.

At the end of our discussion I asked a final question: "What would happen if students did not study the war in school and if teachers never talked about it?"

Their comments convinced me to keep teaching about the war: "Kids won't know what's happening." "Kids will be scared." "Kids will think it's OK to go to war." "Kids are going to hate the people from the Middle East." "Kids will grow up hating, and it will not matter to them if there are wars." "Kids are going to think that death and war are good and normal."

People who argue that we should not teach about "political" issues need to realize that our silence on these issues teaches, too.

The silence of my high school teachers taught me that it was acceptable not to be informed about why the United States was waging war on Iraq, and that it was OK not to have an opinion. Their silence taught me that hating foreigners was OK and that hateful actions toward Arab Americans were normal in the midst of a war against Arabs in the Middle East.

It takes courage to teach about controversial current issues. But what if we don't? ▪

Kelley Dawson Salas (kdsalas@sbcglobal.net) is a Milwaukee teacher and Rethinking Schools editor.

A Revolution of Values

DR. MARTIN LUTHER KING JR.

On April 4, 1967, exactly one year before his assassination, Rev. Martin Luther King Jr. delivered a speech at New York City's historic Riverside Church to the organization Clergy and Laymen Concerned About Vietnam. The speech, titled "Beyond Vietnam," was his first major speech on the war in Vietnam— what the Vietnamese call the American War. In these excerpts, King links the escalating U.S. commitment to that war with its abandonment of the commitment to social justice at home. His call for a "shift from a 'thing-oriented' society to a 'person-oriented' society" and for us to "struggle for a new world" has acquired even greater urgency than when he issued it decades ago.

—The Editors

Now, it should be incandescently clear that no one who has any concern for the integrity and life of America today can ignore the present war. If America's soul becomes totally poisoned, part of the autopsy must read Vietnam. It can never be saved so long as it destroys the deepest hopes of men the world over. So it is that those of us who are yet determined that "America will be" are led down the path of protest and dissent, working for the health of our land....

The war in Vietnam is but a symptom of a far deeper malady within the American spirit, and if we ignore this sobering reality we will find ourselves organizing Clergy and Laymen Concerned committees for the next generation. They will be concerned about Guatemala and Peru. They will be concerned about Thailand and Cambodia. They will be concerned about Mozambique and South Africa. We will be marching for these and a dozen other names and attending rallies without end unless there is a significant and profound change in American life and policy....

In 1957 a sensitive American official overseas said that it seemed to him that our nation was on the wrong side of a world revolution. During the past 10 years we have seen emerge a pattern of suppression that now has justified the presence of U.S. military "advisors" in Venezuela. This need to maintain social stability for our investments accounts for the counterrevolutionary action of American forces in Guatemala. It tells why American helicopters are being used against guerrillas in Colombia and why American napalm and Green Beret forces have already been active against rebels in Peru.

It is with such activity in mind that the words of the late John F. Kennedy come back to haunt us. Five years ago he said, "Those who make peaceful revolution impossible make violent revolution inevitable." Increasingly, by choice or accident, this is the role our nation has taken, the role of those who make peaceful revolution impossible by refusing to give up the privileges and the pleasures that come from the immense profits of overseas investments. I am convinced that if we are to get on the right side of the world revolution, we as a nation must undergo a radical revolution of values. We must rapidly begin the shift from a "thing-oriented" society to a "person-oriented" society. When machines and computers, profit motives and property rights are considered more important than people, the giant triplets of racism, materialism, and militarism are incapable of being conquered.

A NATION THAT CONTINUES YEAR AFTER YEAR TO SPEND MORE MONEY ON MILITARY DEFENSE THAN ON PROGRAMS OF SOCIAL UPLIFT IS APPROACHING SPIRITUAL DEATH.

A true revolution of values will soon cause us to question the fairness and justice of many of our past and present policies. On the one hand, we are called to play the Good Samaritan on life's roadside, but that will be only an initial act. One day we must come to see that the whole Jericho Road must be transformed so that men and women will not be constantly beaten and robbed as they make their journey on life's highway. True compassion is more than flinging a coin to a beggar. It comes to see that an edifice that produces beggars needs restructuring.

A true revolution of values will soon look uneasily on the glaring contrast of poverty and wealth. With righteous indignation, it will look across the seas and see individual capitalists of the West investing huge sums of money in Asia, Africa, and South America, only to take the profits out with no concern for the social betterment of the countries, and say, "This is not just." It will look at our alliance with the landed gentry of South America and say, "This is not just." The Western arrogance of feeling that it has everything to teach others and nothing to learn from them is not just.

A true revolution of values will lay hand on the world order and say of war: "This way of settling differences is not just." This business of burning human beings with napalm, of filling our nation's homes with orphans and widows, of injecting poisonous drugs of hate into the veins of peoples normally humane, of sending men home from dark and bloody battlefields physically handicapped and psychologically deranged, cannot be reconciled with wisdom, justice, and love. A nation that continues year after year to spend more money on military defense than on programs of social uplift is approaching spiritual death.

These are revolutionary times. All over the globe men are revolting against old systems of exploitation and oppression and out of the wombs of a frail world new systems of justice and equality are being born. The shirtless and barefoot people of the land are rising up as never before. "The people who sat in darkness have seen a great light." We in the West must support these revolutions....

Our only hope today lies in our ability to recapture the revolutionary spirit and go out into a sometimes hostile world declaring eternal hostility to poverty, racism, and militarism. With this powerful commitment we shall boldly challenge the status quo and unjust mores and thereby speed the day when "every valley shall be exalted, and every mountain and hill shall be made low, and the crooked shall be made straight and the rough places plain."

A genuine revolution of values means in the final analysis that our loyalties must become ecumenical rather than sectional. Every nation must now develop an overriding loyalty to mankind as a whole in order to preserve the best in their individual societies....

Now let us begin. Now let us rededicate ourselves to the long and bitter—but beautiful—struggle for a new world. ■

TEACHING IDEAS

"A Revolution of Values" Speech by Dr. Martin Luther King Jr.

1. Ask students to write the speech that The Rev. Dr. Martin Luther King Jr. might deliver today if he were alive: What would Dr. King have to say about the "war on terrorism"? The wars in Iraq and Afghanistan? The drone attacks in Pakistan (and on the U.S.-Mexican border)? What would Dr. King say about U.S. global policies today? What evidence from his 1967 speech supports your conclusion? What policies would he urge?

2. Dr. King talks about the giant triplet of racism, materialism, and militarism. Ask students to make charts headed with these categories and to list all the ways they see these forces at work today. Ask them to choose racism, materialism, or militarism and design a poster illustrating it.

3. Tell students: Create a dialogue between Dr. King and another individual. It could be you, the president of the United States, a U.S. soldier in Afghanistan, a high school student considering joining the military, or someone you learned about in this unit.

STEPHEN KRONINGER

Christopher Columbus and the Iraq War

BILL BIGELOW
RETHINKING SCHOOLS (Fall 2005)

Almost all my high school students can recite the singsong rhyme—
In fourteen hundred and ninety two,
Columbus sailed the ocean blue.

Most of them—and most of you—can name Columbus' ships: the Niña, Pinta, and Santa Maria. But since I began teaching in 1978, I've never had a student who could name the nationality of the people he encountered: the Taínos.

This fact hints at how the traditional Columbus myth, and much of the curriculum that follows in its wake, has conditioned children to accept without question imperial adventures like the Iraq War.

For many children, the meeting of Columbus and the Taínos is the first time in the formal curriculum they learn about the contact between different cultures—often as early as October of kindergarten year, around Columbus Day. In fact, it's many children's first in-school exposure to the contact between different nations—to foreign policy.

THE TRADITIONAL COLUMBUS MYTH HAS CONDITIONED CHILDREN TO ACCEPT WITHOUT QUESTION IMPERIAL ADVENTURES LIKE THE IRAQ WAR.

From their earliest days in school, students are taught to identify with white Europeans: the explorers, discoverers, and conquerors. The people Columbus "discovers" are incidental to the main tale of heroism—there, but not there. With few exceptions, children's books describe the arrival of Columbus in remarkably similar ways. Here's a typical passage, from *A Picture Book of Christopher Columbus*: "Christopher Columbus and his men rowed ashore. He planted a flag in the sand and claimed the island for Spain. He named it San Salvador."

Missing from this crisp description is a basic question: What right did Columbus have to claim someone else's territory in the name of a faraway empire? The book acknowledges that there were "natives" living there, so why couldn't these natives keep their land? Why couldn't the land be called what it had been called by its inhabitants for perhaps hundreds of years: Guanahani?

This celebration of colonial conquest is at the heart of the Columbus myth. Children learn that global inequality is a fact of life. The world is divided in two—the discoverers and the discovered, the rulers and the ruled, the civilized and the savage, the worthy and the unworthy. And, as children will learn later, the rich and the poor.

What characteristics does Columbus possess that could justify the domination described in kids' books? The books fail to answer this question directly simply because they never raise it. Students are left to answer it themselves, albeit not consciously: Columbus was white, the natives were not; Columbus was Christian, the natives non-Christian; Columbus was armed, the natives had no guns. The answers children generate validate inequality: Some people in the world inherently have more rights than others.

This fundamental global inequality is the ideological underpinning of U.S. involvement in Iraq. As George W. Bush proclaimed in his January 2003 State of the Union address, justifying the impending war against Iraq: "Once again, we are called to defend the safety of our people and the hopes of all mankind....And as we and our coalition partners are doing in Afghanistan, we will bring to the Iraqi people food and medicines and supplies—and freedom."

According to this logic, "we" have the right to invade other nations when we decide they threaten us. We have a right to occupy other countries. We have the right to impose on them whatever form of government we choose—in the name of freedom, of course. We have the right to decide when others are ready to rule themselves, or not.

In learning about a world divided between a righteous, powerful "us" and an inferior, childlike "them," youngsters sometimes learn that there were different categories of "them." Some Taínos cooperated with the Columbus occupation. But some didn't. Here's how one book, *Meet Christopher Columbus*, acknowledges the native insurgency:

> [Columbus'] ships sailed on to the east. In a few days they came to a small bay. Some of the men went ashore to find food. Suddenly more than 50 Indians jumped out from behind the trees. They had bows and arrows. They attacked the men. The men fought back. One Indian was hit by an arrow. Another was badly cut.
> The Indians were surprised by the bravery of Columbus' men. They dropped their bows and ran away.
> These were the only unfriendly Indians that Columbus' crew ever saw.

Notice that the book calls the European invaders "men," but refers to the Taínos simply as Indians. This is Taíno land, but instead the book portrays the Taínos as aggressors: "They attacked the men." In this historical flip-flop, the colonial invaders bravely "fought back."

Thus is born the friendly Indian/unfriendly Indian dichotomy. The good Indians—think Ahmed Chalabi, Iyad Allawi—cooperate with the occupation forces. The bad Indians—think everyone in Fallujah, for example—fight back. The savages. As former President Bush explained, "Our troops know that they're fighting in Iraq, Afghanistan, and elsewhere to protect their fellow Americans from a savage enemy."

And through it all, God is on "our" side. Former President Bush again: "Americans are a free people, who know that freedom is the right of every person and the future of every nation. The liberty we prize is not America's gift to the world, it is God's gift to humanity."

In children's books, Columbus also seeks to share God's gift. As Mary Pope Osborne explains in *The Story of Christopher Columbus*:

> When Christopher Columbus was a child, he always wanted to be like Saint Christopher. He wanted to sail to faraway places and spread the word of Christianity.

Many of us began to encounter today's justifications for U.S. intervention and domination when we were children. Civilized, Christian Westerners bring enlightenment to the unwashed heathens. Good Indians do what they're told. Bad Indians fight back and get what they deserve.

These myths don't help young people think clearly about the world. What's worse is when a country builds its foreign policy on cartoonlike assumptions about social relations. ▪

Rethinking Schools Curriculum Editor Bill Bigelow (bill@rethinkingschools.com) co-edited Rethinking Columbus: The Next 500 Years.

References

Adler, David. *A Picture Book of Christopher Columbus*. New York: Holiday House, 1962.

De Kay, James. *Meet Christopher Columbus*. New York: Random House Books for Young Readers, 2001.

Pope Osborne, Mary. *The Story of Christopher Columbus: Admiral of the Ocean Sea*. New York: Gareth Stevens Publishing, 1997.

MICHAEL DUFFY

Test Prep and the War

Preparing high schoolers for the Regents exam while studying the war in Iraq

JESSICA KLONSKY
RETHINKING SCHOOLS (Spring 2007)

"You keep saying 'we.' Who is 'we' when you are not fighting in Iraq yourself?"

"We have many weapons. Do you feel it would be right for another country to disarm us?"

"If we ignored Saddam Hussein's use of chemical weapons in the past, why do we care now when he isn't using them?"

My students asked these questions—more difficult than those posed by the U.S. media—during a role play in which I pretended to be President George W. Bush giving his 2003 State of the Union address a few months before the United States invaded Iraq.

The mock press conference was part of a unit in which I blended studying about the war with preparing my students for the New York State English Language Arts Regents Exam, which they must pass in order to graduate. Despite the usual misgivings about what I could and should have done better, I felt pleased that I had been able to meld such an important topic with the district's impossible-to-avoid curricular focus on test prep.

I teach 11th-grade English in Brooklyn at a high school serving a low-income, predominantly Latino population. Every year I have to prepare my students, many of whom are English language learners (ELL), for the Regents exam. Because half of the exam is based on nonfiction writing, I decided to create a nonfiction unit that focused on the war while providing opportunities for my students to practice skills they would need for the Regents: summarizing, annotating, note-taking, and

> **I WANTED MY STUDENTS TO SEE THAT THE NEWS WE ARE REGULARLY EXPOSED TO IS NOT TELLING THE WHOLE STORY ABOUT THE WAR.**

responding to nonfiction writing.

The first day of what became an almost monthlong unit, I asked students to write down everything they knew about the war. We then shared the writings aloud, which gave me a sense of the students' level of understanding. Some students thought Iraq was responsible for the 9/11 attacks, while others knew that Osama bin Laden had no relationship with Iraq. Some didn't even know where Iraq was.

Overall, students were overwhelmingly against the war and hostile toward the Bush administration. At the same time, a number were considering joining the military after high school and would undoubtedly end up in Iraq. I felt I had a responsibility to ensure that they would be able to make informed choices about their future after high school.

In almost all of my classes, three reasons for being in Iraq showed up on the students' lists:

1. We are bringing democracy to Iraq.
2. We are stopping terrorism and getting rid of weapons of mass destruction.
3. Our government wants oil and political control over the Middle East.

Before we examined those different reasons, I wanted to address the issue of the media, in particular how to determine whether a news source is reliable.

I asked my students, "How do we know when we are getting the full picture?" I was surprised by the frustration and cynicism in many of their answers: "You can't believe anything the television tells you." "The president says this and somebody else says that. It's impossible to know who to believe."

It was clear that my students needed to see that it was possible to critically evaluate the information they received and to develop informed opinions about the war. I also wanted them to acquire an understanding of the history and politics that led to the war, so they would be aware of the distortions, omissions, and outright lies in much of the U.S. mainstream media coverage.

SUMMARIZING DIFFERENT VIEWPOINTS

One of the most successful media-related lessons involved an exercise comparing two media viewpoints. First I showed the first 20 minutes of *Control Room*, a documentary about Al-Jazeera, the international Arabic-language television network headquartered in Doha, Qatar. Students were shocked by the dead bodies and destruction shown on Al-Jazeera. For many it was the first time they realized that it wasn't just soldiers who died in war.

For homework, students were to find a U.S. newspaper story about the war and summarize it using the Someone-Wants-But-So strategy—a summarizing strategy where students create a string of sentences in order to summarize a text: Students identify the "main player" in a piece of writing (the "someone"), his or her motivation ("wants"), the conflict ("but"), and the resolution ("so"). I hoped summarizing in this way would help students on the upcoming exam, where they will have to summarize unfamiliar information in an essay.

During the following class period, we discussed how the viewpoints differed. Students found that Al-Jazeera was more concerned with Iraqi lives and interests and with opinions in the Arab world. U.S. newspapers, meanwhile, were more concerned with lives of U.S. soldiers and debates within the U.S. government. Although a few students thought that the Arab media "showed the reality of the war...things 'us' Americans are not shown by our media," most were reluctant to say that any news source was more or less reliable than any other. As one student put it, "The Arab news shows things that put Americans in a bad light and American news shows things that put Arabs in a bad light. Each news favors their own."

My goal was not for students to decide that Al-Jazeera was either a better or worse news source than the *New York Daily News* or the Fox Broadcasting Company. Rather, I wanted my students to see that the news we are regularly exposed to is not telling the whole story about the war. In retrospect, there were a number of problems with this exercise. One is that each student looked at a different U.S. article on a different topic (Saddam's trial, the death of a U.S. soldier, etc.) while the Al-Jazeera coverage was about the beginning of the war. Also, I did not carefully distinguish between bias (and its connotations of prejudice and distortion) and point of view, which is present in any reporting. In the future, I would be more targeted in looking at information, perhaps taking a specific situation and comparing media coverage from a number of sources.

ANNOTATING BACKGROUND INFORMATION

It was clear from our look at the news media that my students needed additional background information. I adapted a *Rethinking Schools* lesson, "The United States and Iraq: Choices and Predictions" (see p. 46) by shortening the number of situations from 10 to six and simplifying the language for my ELL students.

Working in pairs, students read each situation and selected the response they thought the U.S. government should take from a list that ranged from "use military force" to "officially criticize actions" to "support with economic and humanitarian aid." I made it clear that I did not want them to decide what our government would most likely do, but what they thought was the right thing to do. I gave the students a brief explanatory paragraph for each situation and students annotated the paragraphs, underlining key ideas and writing their thoughts and questions in the margins. This kind of careful annotation is an important strategy for students when taking the Regents exam.

The next day, I gave students a one-page document with the actual U.S. responses. We went over these as a class, and students continued to annotate. Even with simplified language and working in pairs, many of the less-skilled readers had enormous difficulty working through these adapted texts. With little or no prior knowledge of Middle Eastern history, nor much experience untangling complex geopolitical situations, many

of my students struggled to understand the various interactions among Iran, Iraq, Saudi Arabia, and the United States over the past 25 years. Even so, students drew some important conclusions from trying to decide the right choice for the United States to make in each situation.

Afterward, students wrote in-class personal responses, choosing from a list of questions I provided: How has U.S. policy in Iraq been consistent or inconsistent? How do U.S. government decisions of the past help you answer the questions you have about the current war?

Many students were disgusted with U.S. actions in Iraq. One student wrote, "Helping other people is a great thing but when you're helping people who are trying to hurt others [supplying chemical weapons agents to Iraq during the war with Iran], that makes you as bad as them." Overall, students felt that, historically, the U.S. government had primarily acted to protect its own interests in the region and not to promote human rights or democracy. This led some students to note that in protecting its interests, sometimes the U.S. government had supported Hussein and other times it had attacked him.

NOTE-TAKING AND QUESTIONING

One of the most interesting activities involved watching the documentary film *Fahrenheit 9/11* by Michael Moore. Politically, the documentary provided additional background information and addressed the question of whether the U.S. government's interests are the same as the interests of people living in the United States. Academically, it provided a chance to improve student skills in note-taking and questioning.

As the students watched the film, they kept notes on a graphic organizer I provided. In particular, I had students keep notes on memorable quotes from Moore and the people he interviewed. Because the Regents exam includes a section that requires students to take notes on a passage they hear read aloud but never see, this note-taking practice was especially important.

Afterward, I put some of the lines they selected (along with some of my own) on pieces of chart paper that I hung up around the room (see "Silent Discussion of *Fahrenheit 9/11*," p. 90). I read each quote aloud and then passed out Post-it notes. The students went through a few rounds of responding to the quotes with their Post-its, and then responding to each other's responses, all without speaking. Later, I opened it up to a class discussion by asking for students to speak on anything they had read that struck them deeply. Depending on the class, these discussions spanned a number of topics—from concerns about military recruitment to whether things would be different if we had an African American president.

Fahrenheit 9/11 is a great film for bringing up issues around the causes and the consequences of the war. It explains and documents, using specific people and actual corporations, the ways in which this war has been waged to profit the few at the expense of the many. However, I still wanted my students to develop a critical eye toward sources of information on the war, even ones they might be sympathetic to.

Toward that end, we spent a few class periods looking at logical fallacies such as slippery slope, red herring, ad hominem, and the straw man argument. We practiced identifying these fallacies in situations not related to the war, and then I asked them to think back on the documentary to identify any logical fallacies.

They quickly identified the ad hominem attacks in the form of cheap shots and still photos of the president looking awkward. They saw Moore's mockery of smaller and less powerful countries involved in the "Coalition of the Willing" as a red herring. One student noted that Moore conveniently left out Great Britain from his list of countries in the coalition—a fallacy of omission. Some students also felt that Moore employed a bit of a slippery slope in linking the Bush family's relations with the bin Laden family to an all-out war in Iraq.

Before moving on to the unit's culminating exercise—a mock Regents exam essay—it was time for the students to hear from the president himself.

I pretended I was the president and my students were the media (see "Why Invade Iraq," p. 56). They listened to me read the 2003 State of the Union address while they had a copy in front of them. In the press conference that followed, they asked me questions. In responding, I tried to use a number of logical fallacies, including some from Bush's actual State of the Union speech.

The students thoroughly enjoyed grilling the president, but were also frustrated by their inability to get straight answers. After the press conference, they wrote in-class response papers about their thoughts and opinions on the war. As before the unit began, most were against the war and critical of Bush. But now their opinions were based on a more solid understanding of the war and the history of U.S./Iraq relations.

As one student wrote:

[This unit] has opened up a whole new thing to me, because before I even saw the video [*Fahrenheit 9/11*] on Iraq I was interested, but not as much as I am now. I mean, when I heard that they were bombing Iraq, I didn't realize the deaths and pain the women and children were going through. It opened my eyes.

WRITING EXAM ESSAYS

To end the unit, I created a mock Regents exam essay assignment in which students read a nonfiction essay, examine a chart or graph, and then respond to demonstrate their understanding. I used the format of countless Regents essay exams I have seen over the years and created this situation:

The students in your class are presenting information to each other about the current war in Iraq. Your teacher has asked each student to write a report explaining a specific aspect of the war.

In groups of three or four, my students selected a specific topic about the war from a list that included cultural/ethnic tensions in Iraq, the role of oil, and military recruitment. Each group received an article and a map, chart, or graph about their topic. To understand the materials, students used the summarizing, annotating, note-taking, and questioning techniques we had practiced throughout the unit. Based on this information, they individually crafted a straightforward informational essay.

In some ways, the essay was a letdown as a final assignment because the Regents essay format does not allow students to express their own opinions or to bring in much outside knowledge; this leads to drab, formulaic writing. But I generally felt good about the content we studied in the unit and that my students had been able to practice important skills such as summarizing, note-taking, and annotation.

However, I realized that there was another important difference between our unit and the Regents exam. The Regents exam requires students to read a nonfiction passage on a topic about which they may not have any prior knowledge. In our unit, however, students learned in depth about the topic before they wrote. While this undoubtedly helped students develop their reading comprehension skills, I wonder if it will help them write about possible Regents essay topics such as irrigation. Or the history of vaudeville theater. Or manatees.

Indeed, in this unit my students had the luxury to write about something they cared about and had studied—rather than the Regents approach of writing for 90 minutes on a topic they may care nothing about, or know nothing about. This, of course, brings up the question of what is most important to know how to do before graduating high school.

Overall, I felt this unit engaged students on a topic they were hungry to understand. When I compared their questions at the beginning of the unit to their questions for Bush during the press conference, I saw how they moved from general distrust and cynicism toward very specific questions that showed a more in-depth understanding of the war. And that specificity is essential to overcome generalized feelings of cynicism and hopelessness, not just about the war but other issues, such as racism and poverty, that the war exposes. Being able to understand how history unfolds helps students think about how things might be different and what would need to be done to make changes.

I hope that detailing my experiences with this unit will encourage other teachers to share their ways of dealing with the dreariness of test prep while still keeping their teaching vibrant and their curriculum relevant. ▪

Jessica Klonsky (mayuc@onebox.com) teaches at EBC High School for Public Service-Bushwick in Brooklyn, N.Y.

Resources

Control Room, directed by Jehane Noujaim (Lions Gate, 2003)

Fahrenheit 9/11, directed by Michael Moore (Sony Pictures, 2003)

The National Priorities Project. Provides educational information on the impact of federal tax and spending policies at the community level. nationalpriorities.org. Oversees the costofwar.com site.

Al-Jazeera (English language portal) http://english.aljazeera.net

Global Policy Forum. Good basic information on Iraq,including printable black-and-white maps. globalpolicy.org

CHAPTER 2

The Road to War

©2008 MIKE KONOPACKI

Empire or Humanity

What the classroom didn't teach me about the American Empire

HOWARD ZINN
RETHINKING SCHOOLS (Summer 2008)

With an occupying army waging war in Iraq and Afghanistan, with military bases and corporate bullying in every part of the world, there is hardly a question any more of the existence of an American Empire. Indeed, the once fervent denials have turned into a boastful, unashamed embrace of the idea.

However, the very idea that the United States was an empire did not occur to me until after I finished my work as a bombardier with the Eighth Air Force in the Second World War and came home. Even as I began to have second thoughts about the purity of the "Good War," even after being horrified by Hiroshima and Nagasaki, even after rethinking my own bombing of towns in Europe, I still did not put all that together in the context of an American "Empire."

I was conscious, like everyone, of the British Empire and the other imperial powers of Europe, but the United States was not seen in the same way. When, after the war, I went to college under the G.I. Bill of Rights and took courses in U.S. history, I usually found a chapter in the history texts called "The Age of Imperialism." It invariably referred to the Spanish-American War of 1898 and the conquest of the Philippines that followed. It seemed that American imperialism lasted only a relatively few years. There was no overarching view of U.S. expansion that might lead to the idea of a more far-ranging empire—or period of "imperialism."

I recall the classroom map (labeled "Western Expansion") which presented the march across the continent as a natural, almost biological, phenomenon. That huge acquisition of land called the Louisiana Purchase hinted at nothing but vacant land acquired. There was no sense that this territory had been occupied by hundreds of Indian tribes which would have to be annihilated or forced from their homes—what we now call "ethnic cleansing"—so that whites could settle the land, and later railroads could crisscross it, presaging "civilization" and its brutal discontents.

Neither the discussions of Jacksonian democracy in history courses, nor the popular book by Arthur Schlesinger Jr., *The Age of Jackson*, told me about the Trail of Tears, the deadly forced march of "the five civilized tribes" westward from Georgia and Alabama across the Mississippi, leaving 4,000 dead in their wake. No treatment of the Civil War mentioned the Sand Creek massacre of hundreds of Indian villagers in Colorado just as "emancipation" was proclaimed for black people by Lincoln's administration.

That classroom map also had a section to the south and west labeled "Mexican Cession." This was a handy euphemism for the aggressive war against Mexico in 1846 in which the United States seized half of that country's land, giving us California and the great Southwest. The term "Manifest Destiny" used at that time soon, of course, became more universal. On the eve of the Spanish-American War, the *Washington Post* saw beyond Cuba: "We are face to face with a strange destiny. The taste of Empire is in the mouth of the people even as the taste of blood in the jungle."

The violent march across the continent, and even the invasion of Cuba, appeared to be within a natural sphere of U.S. interest. After all, hadn't the Monroe Doctrine of 1823 declared the Western Hemisphere to be under our protection? But with hardly a pause after Cuba came the invasion of the Philippines, halfway around the world.

IN WARS, THERE IS ALWAYS A DIFFERENCE BETWEEN THE MOTIVES OF THE SOLDIERS AND THE MOTIVES OF THE POLITICAL LEADERS WHO SEND THEM INTO BATTLE.

The word "imperialism" now seemed a fitting one for U.S. actions. Indeed, that long, cruel war—treated quickly and superficially in the history books—gave rise to an Anti-Imperialist League in which William James and Mark Twain were leading figures. But this was not something I learned in university either.

THE "SOLE SUPERPOWER"

Reading outside the classroom, however, I began to fit the pieces of history into a larger mosaic. What at first had seemed like a purely passive foreign policy in the decade leading up to the First World War now appeared as a succession of violent interventions: the seizure of the Panama Canal zone from Colombia, a naval bombardment of the Mexican coast, the dispatch of the Marines to almost every country in Central America, occupying armies sent to Haiti and the Dominican Republic. As the much-decorated Gen. Smedley Butler, who participated in many of those interventions, wrote later: "I was an errand boy for Wall Street."

At the very time I was learning this history—the years after World War II—the United States was becoming not just another imperial power, but the world's leading superpower. Determined to maintain and expand its monopoly on nuclear weapons, it was taking over remote islands in the Pacific, forcing the inhabitants to leave, and turning the islands into deadly playgrounds for more atomic tests.

In his memoir, *No Place to Hide*, David Bradley, who monitored radiation in those tests, described what was left behind as the testing teams went home: "Radioactivity, contamination, the wrecked island of Bikini and its sad-eyed, patient exiles." The tests in the Pacific were followed, over the years, by more tests in the deserts of Utah and Nevada, more than a thousand tests in all.

When the war in Korea began in 1950, I was still study-ing history as a graduate student at Columbia University. Nothing in my classes prepared me to understand American policy in Asia. But I was reading *I. F. Stone's Weekly*. Stone was among the very few journalists who questioned the official justification for sending an army to Korea. It seemed clear to me then that it was not the invasion of South Korea by the North that prompted U.S. intervention, but the desire of the United States to have a firm foothold on the continent of Asia, especially now that the communists were in power in China.

Years later, as the covert intervention in Vietnam grew into a massive and brutal military operation, the imperial designs of the United States became yet clearer to me. In 1967, I wrote a little book called *Vietnam: The Logic of Withdrawal*. By that time I was heavily involved in the movement against the war.

When I read the hundreds of pages of the *Pentagon Papers* entrusted to me by Daniel Ellsberg, what jumped out at me were the secret memos from the National Security Council. Explaining the U.S. interest in Southeast Asia, they spoke bluntly of the country's mo-tives as a quest for "tin, rubber, oil."

Neither the desertions of soldiers in the Mexican War, nor the draft riots of the Civil War, nor the anti-imperialist groups at the turn of the century, nor the strong opposition to World War I—indeed no antiwar movement in the history of the nation—reached the scale of the opposition to the war in Vietnam. At least part of that opposition rested on an understanding that more than Vietnam was at stake, that the brutal war in that tiny country was part of a grander imperial design.

Various interventions following the U.S. defeat in Vietnam seemed to reflect the desperate need of the still-reigning superpower—even after the fall of its powerful rival, the Soviet Union—to establish its dominance everywhere. Hence the invasion of Grenada in 1982, the bombing assault on Panama in 1989, the first Gulf war of 1991. Was George Bush Sr. heartsick over Saddam Hussein's seizure of Kuwait, or was he using that event as an opportunity to move U.S. power firmly into the coveted oil region of the Middle East? Given the history of the United States, given its obsession with Middle Eastern oil dating from Franklin Roosevelt's 1945 deal with King Abdul Aziz of Saudi Arabia and the CIA's overthrow of the democratic Mossadeq government in Iran in 1953, it is not hard to decide that question.

JUSTIFYING EMPIRE

The ruthless attacks of September 11th (as the official 9/11 commission acknowledged) derived from fierce hatred of U.S. expansion in the Middle East and elsewhere. Even before that event, the Defense Department acknowledged, according to Chalmers Johnson's book *The Sorrows of Empire*, the existence of more than 700 American military bases outside of the United States.

Since that date, with the initiation of a "war on ter-rorism," many more bases have been established or expanded: in Kyrgyzstan, Afghanistan, the desert of Qatar, the Gulf of Oman, the Horn of Africa, and wher-ever else a compliant nation could be bribed or coerced.

When I was bombing cities in Germany, Hungary, Czechoslovakia, and France during World War II, the moral justification was so simple and clear as to be be-yond discussion: We were saving the world from the evil of fascism. I was therefore startled to hear from a gunner on another crew—what we had in common was that we both read books—that he considered this "an imperialist war." Both sides, he said, were motivated by ambitions of control and conquest. We argued without resolving the issue. Ironically, tragically, not long after our discussion, this fellow was shot down and killed on a mission.

In wars, there is always a difference between the motives of the soldiers and the motives of the political leaders who send them into battle. My motive, like that of so many, was innocent of imperial ambition. It was to help defeat fascism and create a more decent world, free of aggression, militarism, and racism.

The motive of the U.S. establishment, understood by the aerial gunner I knew, was of a different nature. It was described early in 1941 by Henry Luce, multimil-lionaire owner of *Time*, *Life*, and *Fortune* magazines, as the coming of "the American Century." The time had arrived, he said, for the United States "to exert upon the world the full impact of our influence, for such purpos-es as we see fit, and by such means as we see fit."

We can hardly ask for a more candid, blunter decla-ration of imperial design. It has been echoed in recent years by the intellectual handmaidens of the Bush ad-ministration, but with assurances that the motive of this influence is benign, that the purposes—whether in Luce's formulation or more recent ones—are noble, that this is an "imperialism lite." As George Bush said in his second inaugural address: "Spreading liberty around the world... is the calling of our time." The *New York Times* called that speech "striking for its idealism."

The American Empire has always been a bipartisan project—Democrats and Republicans have taken turns extending it, extolling it, justifying it. President Woodrow Wilson told graduates of the Naval Academy in 1914 (the year he bombarded Mexico) that the U.S. used "her navy and her army... as the instruments of civilization, not as the instruments of aggression." And Bill Clinton, in 1992, told West Point graduates: "The values you learned here... will spread throughout the country and throughout the world."

For the people of the United States and, indeed, for people all over the world, those claims sooner or later are revealed to be false. The rhetoric, often persuasive on first hearing, soon becomes overwhelmed by horrors that can no longer be concealed: the bloody corpses of Iraq, the torn limbs of American GIs, the millions of families driven from their homes—in the Middle East and in the Mississippi Delta.

Have not the justifications for empire, embedded in our culture, assaulting our good sense—that war is necessary for security, that expansion is fundamental to civilization—begun to lose their hold on our minds? Have we reached a point in history where we are ready to embrace a new way of living in the world, expanding not our military power, but our humanity? ▪

Howard Zinn was the author of SNCC: The New Abolitionists, You Can't Be Neutral on a Moving Train: A Personal History of Our Times, A People's History of the United States, A People's History of American Empire, *and many other books. He died in 2010. Copyright ©2008 Howard Zinn*

Whose Terrorism?

A classroom activity asks students to define terrorism and then apply their definitions to world events

BILL BIGELOW

Shortly after the horrific September 11, 2001, attacks on the World Trade Center and the Pentagon, then-President Bush denounced these as acts of war and proclaimed a "war on terrorism." But what exactly was the target of this war? And what did the president mean by terrorism? Despite uttering the words terror, terrorist, or terrorism 32 times in a September 20 speech to the nation, he never once defined terrorism.

As teachers, we need to engage our students in a deep, critical reading of terms such as terrorism, freedom, patriotism, and "our way of life"—terms that evoke vivid images but can be used for ambiguous ends.

A LESSON ON TERRORISM

I wanted to design a lesson that would get students to surface the definitions of terrorism that they carry around—albeit most likely unconsciously. And I wanted them to apply their definitions to a number of episodes, historical and contemporary, that involved some kind of violence or destruction. I didn't know for certain, but my hunch was that as students applied definitions consistently they would call into question the We're Good/They're Bad dichotomies that have become even more pronounced on the political landscape.

> **"WHEN OUR GOVERNMENT DOESN'T DEFINE TERRORISM, IT MAKES ME THINK THAT THEY JUST WANT A FREE SHOT TO KILL ANYONE THEY WANT."**

I wrote up several "What Is Terrorism?" scenarios, but instead of using the actual names of countries involved, I created fictitious names. Given the widespread conflation of patriotism with support for U.S. government policies, I had no confidence that students would be able to label an action taken by their own government as "terrorism" unless I attached pseudonyms to each country.

For example, in the following scenario I used the example of U.S. support for the Nicaraguan contras in the 1980s. Tobian is the United States, Ambar is Nicaragua, and the country next door is Honduras:

> The government of Tobian is very unhappy with the government of Ambar, whose leaders came to power in a revolution that threw out the former Ambar dictator. Tobian decides to overthrow the new leaders of Ambar. Tobian begins funding a guerrilla army that will attack Ambar from another country next door. So Tobian builds army bases in the country next door and allows the guerrilla army to use its bases. Almost all of the weapons and supplies of the guerrilla army are supplied by Tobian. The guerrillas generally try to avoid fighting the army of Ambar. Instead they

attack clinics, schools, and cooperative farms. Sometimes they mine the roads. Many, many civilians are killed and maimed by the Tobian-supported guerrillas. The guerrillas raid Ambar and then retreat to the Tobian military bases in the country next door.

QUESTIONS:

1. Which, if any, of these activities should be considered "terrorism" according to your definition?
2. Who are the "terrorists"?
3. What more would you need to know to be surer of your answer?

I knew that in such compressed scenarios lots of important information would be missing; hence, I included question No. 3 to invite students to consider other details that might influence their decisions.

Other scenarios included Israeli soldiers taunting and shooting children in Palestinian refugee camps, supported by U.S. military aid; Indian farmers burning Monsanto-supplied, genetically modified cotton crops and threatening to destroy Monsanto offices; the 1998 U.S. cruise missile attack on Sudan's main pharmaceutical plant; and sanctions against Iraq that according to U.N. reports killed as many as a half million children.

DEFINING TERRORISM

Because I was on leave when I developed this lesson, my colleague, Sandra Childs, invited me into her Franklin High School classroom to work with her 11th-grade global studies students. I began by asking students to write down their own personal definitions of terrorism. I wrote the following questions on the board and told students to keep them in mind:

- Does terrorism need to involve the killing of many people or can it affect just one person? Can it involve solely the destruction of property, with no injuries?
- Can governments commit acts of terrorism, or is the term reserved only for people who operate outside of governments?
- Must terrorism involve the people of one country attacking citizens of another country?
- Does motive make a difference?
- Does terrorism need to be intentional?

Immediately following, I explained to students that, in preparation for an activity, I'd like them to get into small groups and read their individual definitions to one another to see if they could build a consensus definition of terrorism. They could choose an exemplary definition from one member or, if they preferred, cobble one together from their separate definitions.

Some groups quickly agreed upon definitions; others would have spent the entire 83-minute class if Sandra and I had let them. In most cases, the definitions were simple but thoughtful. For example, "Intentional acts that create terror, targeted towards a specific group, or innocent people. Not just directly, but indirectly."

I distributed the "What Is Terrorism?" scenarios to students, reviewed the instructions with them, and emphasized that all the scenarios were real. Their main task was to read each situation and to decide whether any of the actions described met their group's definition of terrorism. I gave them permission to approach the situations in whichever order they liked.

Watching students attempt to apply their definitions of terrorism, I was impressed by their eagerness to be consistent. As Sandra and I wandered from group to group, we heard students arguing over whether there was a distinction between oppression and terrorism. Most groups wanted more information on the motives of various actors. Some insisted that if a country supported terrorist acts in another country, then it, too, was a terrorist. Others held that a supporting country could not be held fully responsible for the actions of the actual perpetrators—but if a country knew about terrorism enabled with its funds and did nothing to prevent it, then it, too, was guilty of terrorism.

Although this activity was far too involved to be neatly contained in an 83-minute class, by the end many students came to important insights. One student said, "Ever since they announced that we were going to have a war on terrorism I have wondered who or what a terrorist is. And…it's suspicious that they still haven't defined terrorism." I asked students why they thought the U.S. government had failed to offer a clear definition of terrorism. One student said, "If you don't have any boundaries, then anyone can be a terrorist." Another said, "The U.S. government won't define terrorism because they don't want to be able to be considered terrorists."

These comments echoed the scholar Eqbal Ahmad's insight that countries that have no intention of being consistent will resist defining terms. As one student wrote after the activity: "I also realized how many terrorism acts the United States has committed. When our government doesn't define terrorism, it makes me think that they just want a free shot to kill anyone they want." Wrote another student: "Bush needs to define terrorism in front of our nation before he does anything else, and then he needs to stick with the definition, not bend it to suit the United States."

But then there was this student comment: "I, myself, am really tired of hearing about it. If I go to war, so what, I'll fight for my country. What does this have to do with global studies?" And this young man: "I feel if we don't get our revenge against these 'terrorists' it will diminish the trust of our nation towards our government."

These remarks reminded me of being in the classroom during the fall of 1990, after Iraq had invaded Kuwait and the United States was assembling its military attack force. Many students resisted critical analysis, sensing that critique eroded the patriotic unity then building in the country—that appending a "not so fast" onto the flag-waving interrupted a sense of collective purpose that felt good to many of them. At least that was how I read some students' resistance. During times of war, students may regard even the mildest critical examination of government policy as unpatriotic or even subversive. Nonetheless, I was impressed by how many students in Sandra's classes appeared eager to question their government's framing of key issues.

As we wrapped up in one class, Sandra asked a wonderful question: "What difference do you think it would make if students all over the country were having the discussion that we're having today?"

There were two quick answers before the bell rang: "I'd feel a lot better about the United States," and "I think we'd lose a lot of people who'd want to go fight for the country."

My interpretation: The more students understand about the exercise of U.S. power in the world—both military and economic—the less likely they are to want to extend it.

ECONOMIC TERRORISM

After I'd used the "What Is Terrorism?" situations with Sandra's classes, I realized that, with the exception of sanctions, all of them were incidents of direct attacks on civilians or property. Did my examples narrow students' consideration of terrorism?

In her article "Solidarity Against All Forms of Terrorism," Indian environmentalist and scholar Vandana Shiva urges us to embrace a more expansive notion of terrorism. She asks us to consider "economic policies which push people into poverty and starvation as a form of terrorism," such as International Monetary Fund/World Bank-mandated structural adjustment programs that force governments to cut food and medical programs, with the full knowledge of the misery this will engender. In India, Shiva writes:

Fifty million tribals who have been flooded out of their homes by dams over the past 4 decades were also victims of terrorism—they have faced the terror of technology and destructive development. ... The whole world repeatedly watched the destruction of the World Trade Center towers, but the destruction of millions of sacred shrines and homes and farms by forces of injustice, greed, and globalization go unnoticed.

To help students consider whether some situations could be considered economic terrorism, I added several new "What Is Terrorism?" scenarios. One deals with deaths in southern Africa from AIDS where, for instance, international banks have forced the Zambian government to pay annual debt service charges greater than spending on health and education combined. According to the United Nations, life expectancy there will soon drop to 33 years, a level not seen in the Western world since medieval times. Another new scenario focuses on transnational corporations that knowingly pay wages that are insufficient to sustain life.

TERRORISM'S GHOSTS

As many writers and activists, especially from the Third World, pointed out in the wake of September 11, the U.S. government is ill-placed to lecture the world about terrorism. Writing in the British daily *Guardian*, Indian novelist Arundhati Roy offered the perspective of an individual who is on the receiving end of U.S. global power:

> The September 11 attacks were a monstrous calling card from a world gone horribly wrong. The message may have been written by bin Laden (who knows?) and delivered by his couriers, but it could well have been signed by the ghosts of the victims of America's old wars. The millions killed in Korea, Vietnam, and Cambodia; the 17,500 killed when Israel—backed by the U.S.—invaded Lebanon in 1982, the 200,000 Iraqis killed in Operation Desert Storm, the thousands of Palestinians who have died fighting Israel's occupation of the West Bank. And the millions who died in Yugoslavia, Somalia, Haiti, Chile, Nicaragua, El Salvador, the Dominican Republic, Panama, at the hands of all the terrorists, dictators and genocidists whom the American government supported, trained, bankrolled and supplied with arms. And this is far from being a comprehensive list.

It's not our role as teachers to climb on our soapbox to rail about U.S. foreign policy. And yet, without an honest examination of events like those listed by Roy, how can we expect students to maintain any critical perspective on the U.S. "war against terrorism"? Let's clarify with students what precisely we mean by terrorism. And then let's encourage students to apply this definition to U.S. conduct in the world.

Underlying this curricular demand for consistency is the basic democratic, indeed human, premise that the lives of people from one nation are not worth more than the lives of people from another. A Pakistani university student, Nabil Ahmed, expressed this sentiment to the *Christian Science Monitor*: "There is only one way for America to be a friend of Islam. And that is if they consider our lives to be as precious as their own." ■

Bill Bigelow (bill@rethinkingschools.org) is an editor of Rethinking Schools.

What Is Terrorism? Who Are the Terrorists?

INSTRUCTIONS:

Based on the definitions of terrorism that your group came up with, decide

1. Does this situation meet your definition of terrorism?

2. Who are the "terrorists" in the situation?

3. What additional information would you need to know to be surer of your answers? All the facts are true, but the names of countries and peoples have been changed. It may help your group to make a diagram of the situation.

SITUATION #1

Soldiers from the country of Marak surround a refugee camp made up of people from the country of Bragan. The refugee camp is crowded and the people there are extremely poor. Most of the Bragan people in the refugee camp hate the army of Marak, believing that Marak has invaded Bragan, has taken all the best land and resources for themselves, and treats people from Bragan very poorly. Young men in the refugee camp sometimes fire guns at the soldiers.

According to an eyewitness, a reporter from the *New York Times*, Marak soldiers use loudspeakers to call insults into the refugee camp—in the Bragan language. Over the loudspeakers, soldiers shout obscenities and things like, "Son of a whore!" They dare young Bragan boys—sometimes as young as 10 or 11—to come out near the electric fence that separates the refugee camp from a wealthy settlement of Marak citizens. When the boys and young men go near the fence to throw stones or yell at the Marak soldiers, the soldiers use fire on the boys with live ammunition, often killing or maiming them. The reporter was horrified by what he witnessed. In an article for his newspaper, he wrote:

> Children have been shot in other conflicts I have covered—death squads gunned them down in El Salvador and Guatemala, mothers with infants were lined up and massacred in Algeria, and Serb snipers put children in their sights and watched them crumple onto the pavement in Sarajevo—but I have never before watched soldiers entice children like mice into a trap and murder them for sport.

The government of Marak clearly knows about the behavior of their soldiers and does nothing to stop them. Indeed, Marak soldiers so regularly taunt citizens of Bragan that this behavior appears to be the policy of the Marak government. One additional fact: Every year, Marak is given enormous amounts of money and military equipment by the country of Bolaire, which is aware of how these are used by Marak.

What Is Terrorism? Who Are the Terrorists?

INSTRUCTIONS:

Based on the definitions of terrorism that your group came up with, decide

1. Does this situation meet your definition of terrorism?

2. Who are the "terrorists" in the situation?

3. What additional information would you need to know to be surer of your answers? All the facts are true, but the names of countries and peoples have been changed. It may help your group to make a diagram of the situation.

SITUATION #2

Farmers from the country of Belveron are angry at their own government and at a corporation from the country of Paradar. The Belveron government has allowed the Paradar corporation to plant "test" crops of genetically engineered cotton, which produce their own pesticide. Many Belveron farmers worry that the genetically engineered cotton will pollute their crops—as has happened many times in other countries—and will lead to a breed of superpests that will be immune to chemical pesticides and also to the organic pest control methods many poor farmers use. Without growing and selling cotton, the farmers have no way to feed their families. Belveron farmers believe that the Paradar corporation cares only for its own profit and wants to get Belveron farmers "addicted" to genetically engineered cotton seeds—which the corporation has patented—so that the corporation will have a monopoly. Belveron farmers further point out that the corporation has not told farmers that the "tests" on their land are risky and could pollute their nongenetically engineered cotton crops.

Belveron farmers have announced that they will burn to the ground all the genetically engineered cotton crops. They hope to drive the Paradar corporation out of Belveron. Belveron farmers have also threatened to destroy the offices of the Paradar corporation.

What Is Terrorism? Who Are the Terrorists?

INSTRUCTIONS:

Based on the definitions of terrorism that your group came up with, decide

1. Does this situation meet your definition of terrorism?

2. Who are the "terrorists" in the situation?

3. What additional information would you need to know to be surer of your answers? All the facts are true, but the names of countries and peoples have been changed. It may help your group to make a diagram of the situation.

SITUATION #3

The army of Kalimo has invaded the country of Iona, next door. There are a number of refugee camps in Iona with thousands of people living in them. The refugees themselves lost their homes many years before—some in wars with Kalimo—and others were forced out of their homes by Kalimo. The area around the refugee camps is controlled by the Kalimo army. The commander of the Kalimo army sealed off the refugee camps and allowed militias from Iona, who are hostile to the refugees, to enter two refugee camps and slaughter hundreds of people. The killing went on for 40 hours. At least 1800 people were murdered, perhaps more. One additional fact: The army of Kalimo receives a great deal of military aid from the country of Terramar. Terramar learned of the massacre of the refugees in Iona, but did not halt military aid to Kalimo.

What Is Terrorism? Who Are the Terrorists?

INSTRUCTIONS:

Based on the definitions of terrorism that your group came up with, decide

1. Does this situation meet your definition of terrorism?

2. Who are the "terrorists" in the situation?

3. What additional information would you need to know to be surer of your answers? All the facts are true, but the names of countries and peoples have been changed. It may help your group to make a diagram of the situation.

SITUATION #4

A corporation based in the country of Menin has a chemical factory located in the much poorer country of Pungor. One night, huge amounts of poisonous gases from the factory begin spewing out into the area around the factory. Nobody outside the factory was warned because someone in the company had turned off the safety siren. Not until the gas was upon residents in their beds, searing their eyes, filling their mouths and lungs, did the communities surrounding the factory know of their danger. According to one report: "Gasping for breath and near blind, people stampeded into narrow alleys. In the mayhem children were torn from the hands of their mothers, never to see them again. Those who still could were screaming. Some were wracked with seizures and fell under trampling feet. Some, stumbling in a sea of gas, their lungs on fire, were drowned in their own bodily fluids." No one knows how many people died, but perhaps as many as 6,000 that night and in the years after, more than 10,000.

The corporation had begun a cost-cutting drive prior to the disaster: lowering training periods, using low-cost materials, adopting hazardous operating procedures, cutting the number of workers in half. A confidential company audit prior to the accident identified 61 hazards. Nothing was done.

After the tragedy, the corporation concentrated on avoiding liability, sending in its legal team days before a medical team. Company officials lied about the poisonous nature of the chemicals at the plant. To this day the corporation refuses to disclose medical information on the leaked gases, maintaining it to be a "trade secret." The company did pay some of the victims' families. On average, victims received less than $350 from the company—a total loss of 48 cents per share of company stock.

Conditions in this Pungor community are still hazardous: soil and water are still heavily contaminated. Mercury has been found at between 20,000 to six million times the expected levels. In this community, the rate of stillborn infants is three times the national average of Pungor; infant mortality is twice as high as the national average.

What Is Terrorism? Who Are the Terrorists?

INSTRUCTIONS:

Based on the definitions of terrorism that your group came up with, decide

1. Does this situation meet your definition of terrorism?

2. Who are the "terrorists" in the situation?

3. What additional information would you need to know to be surer of your answers? All the facts are true, but the names of countries and peoples have been changed. It may help your group to make a diagram of the situation.

SITUATION #5

The government of Tobian is very unhappy with the government of Ambar, whose leaders came to power in a revolution that threw out the former Ambar dictator. Tobian decides to overthrow the new leaders of Ambar. They begin funding a guerrilla army that will attack Ambar from another country next door. So Tobian builds army bases in the next-door country and allows the guerrilla army to use its bases. Almost all of the weapons and supplies of the guerrilla army are supplied by Tobian. The guerrillas generally try to avoid fighting the army of Ambar. Instead they attack clinics, schools, and cooperative farms. Sometimes they mine the roads. Many, many civilians are killed and maimed by the Tobian-supported guerrillas. The guerrillas raid Ambar and then retreat to the Tobian military bases in the country next door.

What Is Terrorism? Who Are the Terrorists?

INSTRUCTIONS:

Based on the definitions of terrorism that your group came up with, decide

1. Does this situation meet your definition of terrorism?

2. Who are the "terrorists" in the situation?

3. What additional information would you need to know to be surer of your answers? All the facts are true, but the names of countries and peoples have been changed. It may help your group to make a diagram of the situation.

SITUATION #6

Simultaneously, two embassies of the country of Anza were bombed—each in a different country. In one country, 213 people were killed and over 1,000 injured; in the other, 11 people were killed and at least 70 injured. In retaliation, about three weeks later, Anza launched missiles at the capital city of Baltus, destroying a pharmaceutical factory, injuring at least 10 people, and killing one. Anza claimed that this factory was manufacturing chemicals that could be used to make VX nerve gas—although Anza offered no substantial proof of this claim. Anza also claimed that a prominent individual who they link to the embassy bombings was connected to the pharmaceutical factory, although they provided no evidence of this claim, either—and a great deal of evidence exists to prove that there is no link. Baltus pointed out that they expelled the prominent individual two years earlier and vigorously denied that the pharmaceutical plant was producing nerve gas agents. They said that this important factory produced 70 percent of the needed medicines for the people of Baltus—including vital medicines to treat malaria and tuberculosis. They allowed journalists and other diplomats to visit the factory to verify that no chemical weapons were being produced there. Those who visited the factory agreed that the destroyed factory appeared to be producing only medicines. It is not known how many people may have died in Baltus for lack of the medicines that were being produced in that factory. Anza blocked the United Nations from launching the investigation demanded by Baltus.

What Is Terrorism? Who Are the Terrorists?

INSTRUCTIONS:

Based on the definitions of terrorism that your group came up with, decide

1. Does this situation meet your definition of terrorism?

2. Who are the "terrorists" in the situation?

3. What additional information would you need to know to be surer of your answers? All the facts are true, but the names of countries and peoples have been changed. It may help your group to make a diagram of the situation.

SITUATION #7

The year is 2003. At least one million people in the country of Lukin are infected with HIV/AIDS. Between 1991 and 2001, 700,000 people died of AIDS in Lukin. Currently, about 300 people die each day of AIDS-related causes. Largely because of the HIV/AIDS crisis, life expectancy in Lukin is expected to drop from 43 to 33 years. AIDS could be controlled with a combination of drugs, frequently called a drug "cocktail." However, given current drug prices, this could cost as much as $18,000 a year per patient.

This year, Lukin will pay $174 million in interest payments on its debt—most of which will go to two large international banks. This debt was incurred many years ago, by a different government than the current one. The loans were pushed by banks that had huge amounts of money to lend because oil-producing countries had deposited so much of their revenue. As one observer put it, "The banks were hot to get in. All the banks … stepped forward. They showed no foresight. They didn't do any credit analysis. It was wild." The loans benefited the bankers and the rich of Lukin. However, most people in Lukin are poor—the gross national product (GNP) per capita is only $350. The $174 million in interest payments is more than the money Lukin will spend on health care and education combined. Money that could go to pay for HIV/AIDS prevention and treatment instead is being sent to banks in so-called developed countries.

The international banks know about the dire health situation in Lukin. They have allowed Lukin to postpone some debts, but only after Lukin agreed to conditions that gave the banks even greater control over Lukin's economy—for example, requiring Lukin to sell its national bank to private investors. Still, so long as the banks force Lukin to pay interest on its debts, there is no way Lukin can deal effectively with the AIDS crisis. Each day, 300 more people die.

What Is Terrorism? Who Are the Terrorists?

INSTRUCTIONS:

Based on the definitions of terrorism that your group came up with, decide

1. Does this situation meet your definition of terrorism?

2. Who are the "terrorists" in the situation?

3. What additional information would you need to know to be surer of your answers? All the facts are true, but the names of countries and peoples have been changed. It may help your group to make a diagram of the situation.

SITUATION #8

Led by the country of Lomandia, the United Nations waged a war against the country of Moretta, saying that Moretta illegally invaded another nearby country. After Moretta's army was defeated and removed from the country they'd invaded, Lomandia pushed for sanctions against Moretta to force Moretta to prove that it is not producing "weapons of mass destruction" like nuclear bombs or poison gas. The sanctions mean that Moretta is not allowed to trade with other countries in the world. Moretta cannot get spare parts to repair water purification plants damaged by bombing during the war. It cannot get medicines and spare parts for medical equipment. Moretta claims that it has allowed inspections from the United Nations, but Lomandia says that it has not. According to the United Nations approximately half a million children have died as a result of the sanctions. Documents from Lomandia show that it knew that Moretta civilians were dying as a result of water-born diseases. When asked in a television interview about the reports of massive numbers of civilian deaths—perhaps as many as a million people over several years—a high government official from Lomandia said, "It's worth it."

What Is Terrorism? Who Are the Terrorists?

INSTRUCTIONS:

Based on the definitions of terrorism that your group came up with, decide

1. Does this situation meet your definition of terrorism?

2. Who are the "terrorists" in the situation?

3. What additional information would you need to know to be surer of your answers? All the facts are true, but the names of countries and peoples have been changed. It may help your group to make a diagram of the situation.

SITUATION #9

Bartavia is one of the most repressive countries in the world, especially if you are not white. Only whites can vote, only whites can travel freely, only whites can live where they like. Most whites live comfortably, even luxuriously. Conditions for people who are not white are some of the worst in the world. Bartavia imprisons people who organize for change. Torture is widespread. Over the years, there have been numerous massacres of nonwhite Bartavia civilians—sometimes of young children. The main organizations working for change in Bartavia have asked the world not to invest money in Bartavia and not to have economic or cultural relations with the country until it commits itself to change. Nonetheless, many countries continue to do business with Bartavia. One in particular, Sarino, has allowed its corporations to increase their investments in Bartavia from $150 million to $2.5 billion—all this during a period of tremendous violence and discrimination. Who knows how many thousands of people have died—from violence or poverty—as a result of Sarino's actions.

What Is Terrorism? Who Are the Terrorists?

INSTRUCTIONS:

Based on the definitions of terrorism that your group came up with, decide

1. Does this situation meet your definition of terrorism?

2. Who are the "terrorists" in the situation?

3. What additional information would you need to know to be surer of your answers? All the facts are true, but the names of countries and peoples have been changed. It may help your group to make a diagram of the situation.

SITUATION #10

The Sport-King corporation produces athletic equipment sold all over the world. Although the headquarters of Sport-King is in the country of Morcosas, all of its products are manufactured in other countries. Sport-King uses subcontractors to make its products. More than 500,000 people, mostly women, work for these subcontractors in poor countries.

Sport-King has a "code of conduct" that is supposed to ensure that workers are not mistreated by Sport-King's subcontractors. For example, no child laborers are supposed to be hired, no prisoners may be used as workers, workers may not be forced to work more than 60 hours a week. Sport-King's code of conduct specifies that workers must be paid a country's minimum wage. However, it does not say that this minimum wage needs to be a living wage. Even poor country governments admit that the minimum wage is not enough for people to live on. Sport-King says that it pays the legal wage, but it knows that not all its workers can survive on this wage.

Companies like Sport-King locate their factories in countries that don't allow unions, outlaw strikes, and jail workers who demand higher pay and better conditions. In fact, Sport-King chooses to locate its factories in some of the most repressive countries in the world. Human rights groups argue that companies like Sport-King knowingly locate their factories in very repressive places so that workers can more easily be controlled and exploited. These human rights groups argue that companies like Sport-King could easily afford to pay its workers living wages, but, because this would come out of their enormous profits, they choose not to.

Who's Who?

SITUATION 1:

The country of Marak is Israel, Bragan is Palestine, Bolaire is the United States. This particular example is taken from "A Gaza Diary," by Chris Hedges in the October 2001 *Harpers.*

SITUATION 2:

The country of Belveron is India, Paradar is the United States. The corporation is Monsanto. See "We Will Reduce Your Fields to Ashes," in *Rethinking Globalization: Teaching for Justice in an Unjust World.*

SITUATION 3:

Kalimo is Israel, Iona is Lebanon, Terramar is the United States. The refugees are Palestinian. The camps were Sabra and Shatila in 1982. The militia was Christian Phalangist.

SITUATION 4:

The country of Menin is the United States, Pungor is India. The corporation was Union Carbide, in Bhopal, India. The year was 1985.

SITUATION 5:

The country of Tobian is the United States. Ambar is Nicaragua. The country next door is Honduras. The time is the 1980s during the U.S.-sponsored Contra war.

SITUATION 6:

The country of Anza is the United States. Baltus is Sudan. The countries where the U.S. embassies were bombed are Kenya and Tanzania. The prominent individual mentioned is Osama bin Laden.

SITUATION 7:

The country of Lukin is Zambia. The banks are the International Monetary Fund and the World Bank. For more information and lessons on the IMF and the Third World debt crisis, see *Rethinking Globalization: Teaching for Justice in an Unjust World.*

SITUATION 8:

The country of Lomandia is the United States. Moretta is Iraq. The U.S. official quoted was Secretary of State Madeleine Albright, interviewed by Leslie Stahl on *60 Minutes.*

SITUATION 9:

The country of Bartavia is South Africa during apartheid. Sarino is the United States. See *Strangers in Their Own Country: A Curriculum Guide on South Africa.*

SITUATION 10:

Sport-King is Nike, although it could be many transnational corporations. The country of Morcosas is the United States.

Teaching Gulf War II

Lessons that encourage students to question the official story on Iraq

BILL BIGELOW

This article was originally written in early March 2003, shortly before the United States military invaded Iraq. As I sat down that fall to plan how I was going to teach about the impending war, I was struck by how much information was available and yet how little curriculum. What follows are descriptions of a few of the activities I used to encourage my students to question the pro-war barrage from politicians and pundits. I believe they are still useful lessons as background to the current U.S. wars in the region.

CREATING THE "ENEMY"

During the first Gulf War, I showed my students the Popeye video *Ali Baba and the Forty Thieves.* I showed it again, to my global studies students, during the lead-up to the U.S. invasion in 2003. In the cartoon, Popeye the sailor—in this instance, as a member of the U.S. Coast Guard—is pitted against Bluto-as-Abu Hassan, an Arab marauder who rides through the land singing, "Now make no error, I'm called the terror of every village and town—Abu Hassan!" Popeye discovers the bandit hideout and, astonished at Abu Hassan's plunder, announces, "I have to give all these jewels back to the people." After Popeye inhales a can of spinach, his biceps turn into tanks and, while Sousa martial tunes play in the background, Popeye single-handedly pummels Abu Hassan and his band of turban-wearing look-alikes. Afterward, Popeye, Olive Oyl, and Wimpy return enormous piles of loot to faceless, cheering townspeople.

> **I WANTED STUDENTS TO THINK ABOUT THE FRAMEWORKS THAT THE MEDIA FASHIONS FOR US—THE PURELY BAD GUYS AND THE PURELY GOOD GUYS, THE CLEANSING ROLE OF VIOLENCE, THE CONTEMPT FOR NON-WESTERN CULTURES.**

I introduced the cartoon by telling students that I wanted them to think about the images that Americans have absorbed of Arabs and the role of the U.S. military in the world. I read aloud a quote from Ariel Dorfman's book, *The Empire's Old Clothes,* in which he introduces the idea of the "secret education" that children absorb from cartoons, comics, and "industrially produced fiction." I told them: "As you view the cartoon, think about the content of the secret education for the children watching it." On the board I wrote: What does the cartoon teach about good guys and bad guys, the role of the U.S. military in the world, Arabs and Arab culture, men's and women's roles, violence, and how conflict is resolved?

After the video, students wrote briefly on these questions before we talked. One student wrote:

To me, this cartoon is saying that we [the United States, portrayed by Popeye] can do whatever we want to other people in other cultures, because we're always right. Violence is alright and gives you power and control.

And another:

Arab culture and their language are funny and they cannot defend themselves. They need Popeye to come and save them. Women are absent in Arab cultures.

I wanted students to think about the frameworks that the media fashions for us—the purely bad guys and the purely good guys, the cleansing role of violence, the contempt for non-Western cultures. And I wanted them to recognize how we are often led to organize information about today's global conflicts, especially those in the Middle East, into these frameworks.

I drew on this concept later when I showed a six-minute excerpt from the video *Toxic Sludge Is Good for You*, which is about the public relations industry. The video features a segment with Nayirah, a teenage Kuwaiti girl who testified in the fall of 1990 before a Congressional caucus (where witnesses are not under oath) and claimed to have seen Iraqi invaders dumping babies onto the hospital floor as they stole incubators. It was an arresting, heart-wrenching story, and politicians and the news media repeated it again and again during the buildup to the first Gulf War. Then-President George H.W. Bush told this story in public several times. The only problem: It was totally fabricated. Nayirah was the daughter of the Kuwaiti ambassador to the United States, and the entire charade was orchestrated by the giant U.S. public relations firm Hill and Knowlton. I wanted students to think about how Americans' secret education prepared them to believe Nayirah's testimony without any other corroborating evidence. I asked students to consider why it was only many months later that Nayirah's claim was discovered to be untrue—why Congress and the press didn't greet her story with more skepticism.

BUSH'S BLANK CHECK

George W. Bush's authority to make war on Iraq derived from a joint resolution that Congress passed early in 2003 that gave the then-president a virtual blank check. In the weeks leading up to the resolution's passage, many commentators remarked that this was the most sweeping military authority given a president since the 1964 Tonkin Gulf Resolution. We now know that the Tonkin resolution, opposed by no U.S. representatives and only two senators, was based on half-truths and outright lies (the resolution is available online at http://en.wikisource.org/wiki/Gulf_of_Tonkin_Resolution).

I decided to pair the resolutions in a lesson. I distributed the Gulf of Tonkin resolution to students and briefly reviewed some of the background about North Vietnam and South Vietnam, but without giving any of the specific circumstances leading up to the alleged attacks on the U.S. destroyer Maddox. I asked students to work in pairs, to imagine that they were members of Congress when this resolution was introduced in 1964, and to come up with at least five critical questions that they would have wanted fully answered before they voted on the resolution. I explained the structure of the resolution as an upside-down essay, with each "whereas" intended as a piece of evidence supporting the thesis, i.e., the resolution.

My students were much more critical and inquisitive than the compliant members of Congress who voted Lyndon Johnson vast war-making powers in 1964. They asked things like: "How do we know that the attacks were part of a 'deliberate and systematic campaign of aggression'?" "What damage did the alleged attacks cause?" "What is the history of U.S. involvement in Vietnam?"

I then shared with them information about what had actually happened in the Gulf of Tonkin in 1964 and why Senate Foreign Relations Committee Chairman J. W. Fulbright later called Johnson a liar for what he had told Congress.

I wanted students to carry this critical stance into an examination of the Iraqi invasion resolution that the Bush administration sought from Congress. The Bush resolution (available at http://usgovinfo.about.com/library/weekly/bliraqreshouse.htm and other sites) is much longer than the Tonkin resolution, with 16 "whereas" clauses, so I divided the class into eight groups. I asked students to assume the same personas as in the Tonkin exercise: skeptical members of Congress. Each group was responsible for looking carefully at a different set of two clauses and coming up with at least one critical question for each "whereas." Everyone needed to examine the concluding "authorization of United States Armed Forces" section and decide on at least one critical question in response. Finally, I asked students to indicate any issues that were not addressed in the resolution. Note that many of the Bush clauses refer to U.N. Security Council resolutions—many of them passed during the seven months in 1990-91 when Iraq occupied

Kuwait. (These can be found at the U.N. web site www. un.org. Click on Documentation, then Security Council Resolutions. Resolutions are listed by year.)

I was surprised—and pleased—that students were able to be so critical of the Bush resolution. It was my first clue that there was widespread skepticism among students about the Bush claims. Based on their knowledge of the Tonkin Gulf lies, most of their questions centered on the lack of evidence provided in the resolution: "What proof do we have that Iraq is harboring terrorists?" "What does Iraq have to say?" "How is Iraq threatening the national security interests of the U.S.?" "What exactly are the national security interests of the U.S.?" and "Why doesn't this resolution say anything about oil?"

SILENT WAR OF SANCTIONS

From 2003 up through today, the focus of debate about US policy on Iraq has been on the invasion and occupation. I wanted my students to recognize that in many respects the United States was already at war with Iraq. I showed the video *Greetings from Missile Street*, which is about several members of the solidarity organization Voices in the Wilderness who spent the summer of 2000 in Basra, in southern Iraq. These individuals chose the hottest months, when temperatures can hit 120° or even 130°. They wanted to experience the impact of sanctions from the standpoint of ordinary Iraqis. To my knowledge, this is the best classroom resource on sanctions; unfortunately it is now difficult to find. The video has a bit of a home movie feel to it: We listen to several Voices in the Wilderness members talk about their Basra experiences against the backdrop of images of family and community life there. It's too bad that we don't hear more from Iraqis themselves. Nonetheless, the video has an intimacy that clearly had an impact on my students. In his reaction paper after the video, one student wrote:

> After awhile I start to think every Middle East person is just as evil as Saddam Hussein. What I saw on *Greetings from Missile Street* almost shocked me. I can truly say that it was the first time I haven't seen an Iraqi person burn an American flag or chant "Down USA!" For the first time I saw "them" as humans.

The video also includes the clearest and most detailed explanation that I've seen about the operation of the U.N. 661 Committee, the group that actually administered the sanctions and decided which items Iraq could or could not import. Operating by "consensus," the 661

Committee rules allowed the United States to block the importation of countless items into Iraq—including blood bags, ambulances, and parts to rebuild Iraq's water treatment plants, destroyed by U.S. bombing in 1991. It is apparent that these were not U.N.-imposed sanctions as much as they are U.S.-imposed sanctions.

I introduced the video by telling students that we were going to watch a film that was made illegally. I talked briefly about the initial imposition of sanctions on Iraq shortly after the Iraqi invasion of Kuwait in August of 1990, and asked them to take notes on all the effects of sanctions that they could find—on physical and psychological health, sanitation, economy, education.

After watching the video, I gave students the choice to write on several questions:

- What would motivate U.S. citizens to risk so much in traveling to Iraq in violation of U.S. law? Try to imagine the kinds of experiences that these individuals had that would lead them to make this choice.
- In the video, *60 Minutes* correspondent Leslie Stahl asks then-U.N. Ambassador Madeleine Albright about the thousands upon thousands of deaths that have been attributed to sanctions, and whether or not it was worth it. Albright indicates that it's a difficult issue, but that it was worthwhile. Why do you think that Albright and other U.S. government officials believe this? (Choose an Iraqi individual you encountered in the video or one of the U.S. members of Voices in the Wilderness, and write a conversation between this individual and Albright.)
- One of the U.S. justifications for invading Iraq involves "weapons of mass destruction." Why do some people consider sanctions to be a "weapon of mass destruction"? What if anything distinguishes this weapon of mass destruction from others?
- What did you learn about Iraq and Iraqi people that you didn't know before? What surprised you, intrigued you, saddened you, angered you?

Many students found the video disturbing—how could their government knowingly participate in denying people clean water or needed medicines? "This video saddened my heart," one girl wrote. But others were angry: "I just want to stand up taller than any building and tell everyone what is happening," wrote another. I was encouraged by how many students drew hope from the big-hearted defiance of the Voices in the Wilderness members: "They are the true heroes of America," wrote one girl. "I think it's people like them that make the

United States not seem like a completely selfish country." Another student wrote: "I'm so proud to be an American when I see Americans like them making a difference." Two valuable, student-friendly articles on the sanctions that could accompany the video are:

- "Iraqi Sanctions: Without Medicines and Supplies, the Children Die," by Matthew Hay Brown. Brown's article is an especially good match with *Greetings from Missile Street* because it, too, describes life in Basra in 2000. It's relatively short, accessible, and moving.

- "What Happens to Your Heart," by David Morse. This also pairs well with *Missile Street* because it focuses on how people are themselves transformed by working in defiance of the economic sanctions. As one Canadian, Rick McCutcheon, says of his work in Iraq: "My heart had just filled with that darkness for many years. And then it just breaks open. And there in the midst of this suffering, is light." It's through exposure to the work of solidarity workers like these that students can learn about the horrific consequences of U.S. foreign policy without being defeated by that knowledge.

WHY WAR?

There I was, feeling my way along, trying to piece together a curriculum that would urge students to think critically about the antecedents to the coming war. The most important question wandered in and out of these lessons but still remained to be confronted directly in my classroom: Why? Why was the United States so intent on overthrowing Saddam Hussein? Why in 2003? Why not other oppressive regimes, like China? Why not other nations in violation of U.N. Security Council resolutions, like Israel? Why not other nations which, unlike Iraq, are known definitively to possess weapons of mass destruction, like Pakistan? Why not other nations with alleged links to terrorists, like Saudi Arabia?

Clearly, if the welfare of the Iraqi people were uppermost in U.S. policymakers' minds as they contemplated invasion, then it's unlikely that the deaths of hundreds of thousands of children through sanctions would have been deemed "worth it." A fuller explanation would need to engage students in exploring the central role that Iraq's oil—proven reserves second only to Saudi Arabia—plays in this conflict. For example, what impact does a U.S.-controlled Iraq have on the power of OPEC? But Iraq is also a water-rich country in a water-poor

region. What role does water play in U.S. war plans? The video *Hidden Wars of Desert Storm* discusses ways in which the Saddam bogeyman benefited U.S. elite interests—for example, by convincing the Saudis to allow U.S. troops to be permanently stationed in their country and boosting U.S. arms sales in the region. And, as we saw vividly in the 2002 elections, saber rattling abroad distracts attention from domestic misery and malfeasance.

This is not the time for social justice educators to hole up in our classrooms and play curricular lone rangers. The issues are too complicated, the pedagogical challenges too stiff. Let's join together in teacher study groups, anti-war teach-ins, and curriculum fairs; and share insights and dilemmas on critical teaching listservs. Now, more than ever, we need each other. ▪

Bill Bigelow (bill@rethinkingschools.org) is an editor of Rethinking Schools.

Resources

Brown, Matthew Hay. "Iraqi Sanctions: Without Medicines and Supplies, the Children Die," *Hartford Courant*, Oct. 23, 2000, online at www.commondreams.org/views/102300-103.htm.

Dorfman, Ariel. *The Empire's Old Clothes: What the Lone Ranger, Babar, and Other Innocent Heroes Do To Our Minds.* London: Penguin: 1996

Ellsberg, Daniel. *Secrets; A Memoir of Vietnam and the Pentagon Papers.* Viking Adult: 2002. A personal and engaging account of the Gulf of Tonkin events.

Gettleman, Marvin, Jane Franklin, Marilyn Young, and H. Bruce Franklin, eds., *Vietnam and America: A Documented History.* Grove Press, 1995. An excellent reader for more background on the Tonkin Gulf Resolution.

Morse, David. "What Happens to Your Heart," *Yes! Magazine*, Spring 2002, available online at www.yesmagazine.org/issues/what-does-it-mean-to-be-an-american-now/what-happens-to-your-heart.

Ali Baba and the Forty Thieves is available at http://www.archive.org/details/PopeyeAliBaba.

Hidden Wars of Desert Storm, Free Will Productions DVD, www.hiddenwars.com.

Toxic Sludge Is Good for You is available at www.mediaed.org/cgi-bin/commerce.cgi?preadd=action&key=119

The U.S. and Iraq: Choices and Predictions

BY HYUNG NAM

This lesson looks back at the history of U.S. relations with Iraq in order to shed light on U.S. objectives at the beginning of the war against Iraq in 2003. Students focus on critical choice points in U.S. policy on Iraq. As they predict policy choices, they not only learn what happened historically that led to the war, but also understand that there were real possibilities for creating a different policy.

Students may be disturbed to learn much of this information, which has been omitted or overlooked in the typical portrayals of U.S.-Iraqi relations. During this lesson, invite students to reflect on why this information is not common knowledge and encourage students to find alternative sources of information.

The lesson will take two to three class periods.

SUGGESTED PROCEDURE

1. Inform students that they will examine crucial choice-points of U.S. leaders. They will predict how the United States responded in each case, and explain the likely rationale of U.S. leaders. Tell students that they will later learn what the real decisions were.

2. Put students in groups of three and distribute copies of "U.S. Government Response Options." Go through the options, and make sure they understand each one. For instance, you may need to explain economic sanctions: "Sanctions are a way to pressure a government to change its policy or to pressure a people to rise up against the government. Sanctions forbid other countries from doing business with the targeted country, or from selling or buying particular goods from them."

3. Distribute copies of "Iraq Situation #1." Ask students to examine the first problem. Have them discuss it in their small groups, then individually write their group's prediction and the likely reasons for it. For the first few situations, make time for students to share their group's prediction and rationale with the large class. This helps students get an idea of the range of possible predictions and rationales, and they may discover that their predictions are similar. Don't let students know what really happened until they have finished all 10 predictions.

4. Distribute "Iraq Situation #2." Have students follow the same procedure, making predictions for the situation, writing individually, and then sharing with the full class. Hearing other students' responses may reassure them that their predictions are not unreasonable.

Materials Needed:

1. Copies of "U.S. Government Response Options"—one for each group.

2. Copies of each "Iraq Situation" (1-10)—one for each student.

3. Copies of "The U.S. and Iraq: Discussion Questions"—one for each student.

4. Copies of "U.S. Government Responses on Iraq"—one for each student.

5. Continue with the remaining situations, although you'll want to stop the full-class sharing time as soon as you feel that everyone understands the assignment. (This can take one and a half to two class periods.)

6. After students have finished all 10 problems, distribute copies of "The U.S. and Iraq: Discussion Questions." Preview the questions, explaining that they will need to write on them in preparation for the discussion. You may choose to have students write longer pieces on only one or two. You may also choose to have them discuss before they write.

7. Distribute copies of "U.S. Government Responses on Iraq." As you read them aloud together, tell students to highlight and take notes on essential information to help them on the writing assignment. After sharing each response, briefly have a few students compare the real decisions with their predictions.

8. Assign the "Discussion Questions" for written homework, and then use them to guide a discussion the next day. You may later wish to use these questions to generate persuasive essay topics. Combining questions 1 and 3 to write an essay on the consistency or inconsistency of U.S. foreign policy encourages students to grapple with the apparent inconsistency of particular policy responses in the context of maintaining U.S. influence and dominance in the region.

RECOMMENDED EXTENSIONS

Return to the present day to examine the current U.S. policy and how oil is an important factor. Many people, including prominent government officials of U.S. allies, have accused U.S. leaders of wanting to go to war with Iraq for oil. Examine data on oil exports from the Middle East. Point out that the majority of oil from the Middle East is exported to Japan, Europe, and other parts of Asia and Africa. In light of these issues, have students critically revisit former President George H.W. Bush's appeal, "Our jobs, our way of life, our own freedom and the freedom of friendly countries around the world will suffer if control of the world's great oil reserves fall in the hands of one man, Saddam Hussein." ▪

Hyung Nam (hnam@pps.k12.or.us) teaches at Wilson High School in Portland, Ore.

References and Resources

Blum, William. "Iraq 1990-1991: Desert Holocaust," in *Killing Hope: US Military and CIA Intervention Since WWII*. Common Courage Press, 1995.

Dickey, Christopher and Thomas, Evan. "Supporting Saddam: The US Helped Build Up the Leader It Now Seeks to Oust," *Newsweek/MSNBC* 9/23/02. www.globalpolicy.org/component/content/article/167/34978.html

Dobbs, Michael. "US Had Key Role in Iraq Buildup, " in *Washington Post*, 12/30/02.

"Gulf War," *Frontline*. www.pbs.org/wgbh/pages/frontline/gulf/script_a.html

Institute for Policy Studies. "Detailed Analysis of October 7 Speech by Bush on Iraq" reprinted at www.commondreams.org/views02/1009-10.htm

Kay, Katty. "Analysis: Oil and the Bush Cabinet" news.bbc.co.uk/2/hi/americas/1138009.stm. 2001 (Uses the National Security Archives to examine U.S. support for Saddam Hussein with primary document analysis of declassified memos and documents released under the Freedom of Information Act.)

Klebnikov, Paul. "Hitting OPEC by Way of Baghdad," at www.globalpolicy.org/component/content/article/185/40492.html. 2002

OPLAN 1002. *Defense of the Arabian Peninsula* (Information on U.S. military objectives and planning in the Middle East before Gulf War I) www.globalsecurity.org/military/ops/oplan-1002.htm

Scahill, Jeremy. "The Saddam in Rumsfeld's Closet." www.commondreams.org/views02/0802-01.htm

"Shaking Hands with Saddam Hussein: the U.S. Tilts toward Iraq, 1980-1984," in *National Security Archive Electronic Briefing Book No. 82.* www.gwu.edu/~nsarchiv/NSAEBB/NSAEBB82/ (Has links to declassified documents and photo and video clips of Rumsfeld shaking Hussein's hand.)

Zunes, Stephen. *Foreign Policy in Focus Special Report #12—The Gulf War: Eight Myths.* www.fpif.org/articles/the_gulf_war_8_myths

Ungerman, Gerard. *Hidden Wars of Desert Storm.* Free Will Productions. www.hiddenwars.com

Graham-Brown, Sarah, and Toensing, Chris. "Why Another War? A Backgrounder on the Iraq Crisis, 2nd Ed." Middle East Research and Information Project. www.why-war.com/files/iraq_background2_merip.pdf

Paul, James "Iraq: the Struggle for Oil" www.globalpolicy.org/component/content/article/185/40471.html. 2002

U.S. Government Response Options

Predict how the U.S. government will respond in each case and explain the likely reasons for its decisions. Range of possible options can include changes or additions to one or more of the following:

- Use military force
- Use economic sanctions (prohibitions on the purchase, sale, or distribution of certain goods to targeted country) to discourage undesirable behavior
- Officially criticize actions
- Ignore the actions
- Support with military aid (money, training, equipment, or personnel)
- Support with economic and humanitarian aid
- Other response (explain)

Iraq Situations

SITUATION #1 (1982): IRAN-IRAQ WAR

Iraq is now in the second year of war against Iran, its neighboring count[...]
recently overthrew the shah, the ruler of Iran, who was supported by th[...]
C.I.A. U.S. officials are concerned that if Iran begins to dominate the reg[...]
Shiite Muslim factions could spread to pro-U.S. oil-rich countries such as[...]
Some U.S. officials are considering taking Iraq off the list of sponsors of[...]
Congress object. The U.S. is considering selling weapons to Iraq in order to prevent Iranian power and
influence in this region. What will the U.S. government do?

SITUATION #2 (1983): IRAQ USES CHEMICAL WEAPONS AGAINST IRAN

Donald Rumsfeld, President Reagan's special envoy (who will later become President George W. Bush's
secretary of defense), meets with Saddam Hussein. Rumsfeld knows that Hussein has been working
on nuclear weapons. In 1984 Rumsfeld meets again with Hussein right after reports that the Iraqi
military is using chemical gas almost every day against Iranian soldiers. Iraq had been losing the war
against Iran up until then. (The use of chemical weapons was outlawed by the 1925 Geneva Protocol
as weapons of mass destruction.) Some members of the U.S. government want to allow Iraq to buy
equipment including computers, dual-use chemicals, anthrax bacteria, and helicopters. They also
consider giving satellite information to Iraq to aid them in their fight against Iran. How will the U.S.
government respond to reports of Iraq's use of chemical weapons?

SITUATION #3 (1988): IRAQ USES BANNED WEAPONS AGAINST THE KURDS

Hussein orders his military to drop bombs with poisonous mustard gas, sarin, VX gas, and tabun
against the Kurds (an ethnic minority group) in northern Iraq. Hussein's cousin in the government,
known as "Chemical Ali," says, "Who is going to say anything? The international community?" Many
officials in Congress, the State Department, and White House are concerned about Saddam's use of
banned weapons. The U.S. Senate considers a resolution that proposes sanctions against Iraq. What will
the U.S. government do?

SITUATION #4 (JULY 1990): IRAQ THREATENS KUWAIT

Saddam Hussein accuses Iraq's neighbor, Kuwait, of drilling $2.4 billion worth of Iraqi oil at the
border between Iraq and Kuwait while it was locked in war with Iran and also of bringing down the
international price of oil by overselling. Iraq argues that this practice caused its treasury to lose billions
of dollars while it was desperately in debt from war. Saddam calls this an "economic war" and demands
$10 billion in compensation, threatening to go to war against Kuwait. The Kuwaiti government ignores
these demands and Saddam amasses troops at the border.

Knowing that the U.S. government sees Kuwait as a friend in the region, Saddam checks to learn
the U.S. stance on his threat to invade Kuwait. The U.S. ambassador, April Glaspie, tells him: "We're
watching you. We're concerned about the bellicose statements that you've been issuing. But our
fundamental feeling is that we have no direct vested interest in Arab-Arab disputes, including the
dispute that you're having with the Kuwaitis over the mutual border that you share." Is Saddam
confused about whether the United States will take a stand on this dispute? Will the United States help
settle the conflict to help maintain peace in the Middle East? Will it clearly warn Saddam not to invade?

TION #5 (AUG. 2, 1990): IRAQ INVADES KUWAIT

...ter negotiation, the Iraqis walk out on talks when the Kuwaitis refuse to meet their demands. Saddam Hussein invades Kuwait. The United Nations Security Council and the Arab League immediately condemn the Iraqi invasion. Four days later, in Resolution 661, the U.N. Security Council imposes an economic embargo on Iraq that prohibits nearly all trade with Iraq. Iraq responds to the sanctions by annexing [taking over] Kuwait on August 8, prompting the exiled Kuwaiti monarchy to call for a stronger international response. With control of Kuwait, Saddam has control of one-fifth of the world oil supplies. Saddam indicates that he is willing to negotiate a withdrawal from Kuwait in exchange for his demands. Arab countries want a chance to mediate in order to resolve the conflict peacefully. Many U.S. citizens are wary of another war after the experience of Vietnam. There are many in Congress who also question the idea of going to war. Will the United States try to negotiate a diplomatic solution or prepare to go to war against Iraq's invasion?

SITUATION #6 (JAN. 17, 1991): IRAQI WATER AND ELECTRICAL FACILITIES TARGETED

The United States is leading the U.N. coalition in a war to make Saddam's troops retreat from Kuwait. Iraq's infrastructure for clean water, sanitation, and electrical power is an essential life support for the country. The U.S. Defense Intelligence Agency considers the strategy of extensively bombing Iraqi infrastructure, predicting a huge impact on Iraqi civilians. Children will be the most in danger of sickness and death from diarrhea and acute respiratory infections. U.S. government studies after World War II had concluded that "the dread of disease and hardships imposed by the lack of sanitary facilities were bound to have a demoralizing effect upon the civilian population," and that there was a "reliable and striking correlation between the disruption of public utilities and the willingness of the German population to accept unconditional surrender." Will the U.S. government attack Iraqi water and electrical facilities?

SITUATION #7: (JANUARY 1991) DEPLETED URANIUM

The United States and Great Britain prepare to attack Iraq in order to force Iraqi troops out of Kuwait. There is a new and powerful weapon at their disposal: tank and rocket shells made in part from depleted uranium 238, a metal 1.7 times denser than lead. These shells can pierce armor—including tanks. In fact, they cut through armor "like a hot knife through butter." The problem with this weapon is that depleted uranium creates a fine aerosol-like radioactive and chemically toxic dust. And it doesn't ever go away; it has a half-life of 4.5 billion years. U.S. military studies indicate that use of depleted uranium 238 on the battlefield could lead to cancers of the lung and bone, kidney damage, nonmalignant lung disease, neurocognitive disorders, chromosomal damage, and birth defects. Use of depleted uranium shells could not only contaminate Iraqi soldiers and Iraqi and Kuwaiti civilians, it could also poison the tens of thousands of U.S. and British troops who will attack the Iraqi military after depleted uranium shells have been used. Will the U.S. military use depleted uranium shells, warn the troops, and equip them with special masks to avoid contamination? Will they use the shells but not warn their troops? Will they decide not to use depleted uranium weapons? What will the U.S. government do?

SITUATION #8 (MARCH 1991): SHIITE-KURD REBELLION

Iraqi troops have now retreated from Kuwait. Shiites in southern Iraq and Kurds in the north rebel against Saddam. The U.S. government is concerned that if Shiites in Iraq gain power, they might join with Shiites in Iran and strengthen their influence in a region that has 65 percent of the world's oil supply. The U.S. government considers returning captured helicopters and weapons to the Iraqi military controlled by Saddam Hussein. He might use these weapons against the rebels. What will the U.S. government do?

SITUATION #9 (1998): SANCTIONS HURT CIVILIANS

The U.N. Children's Fund (UNICEF) releases a report indicating that the sanctions (started in 1991 to pressure Iraq to disarm weapons of mass destruction) have resulted in the deaths of more than half a million Iraqi children (5,000 per month) and that 250 Iraqis die each day as a result of the sanctions. After almost eight years of sanctions, Saddam Hussein has not met all requirements to disarm. Iraq's national economy has shrunk to one-fifth of its size in 1979, but Saddam continues to rule and maintain his many palaces while Iraqi civilians suffer. Conditions in Iraq include untreated sewage, no clean water, shortages of food and medicine, and highly inflated prices for everything. According to the Geneva Conventions, civilians are not to be targeted by war or economic sanctions. What will the U.S. government do?

SITUATION #10: (1998-2002): NO-FLY ZONE

Without U.N. authority, the United States and Britain have been patrolling and bombing in "no-fly zones" in Iraq, saying that they patrol these regions to protect the lives of minority groups that Saddam Hussein might threaten. The United States and Britain engage in almost daily attacks on Iraqi anti-aircraft emplacements. They launch major bombing episodes in response to alleged "significant movements" of Iraqi armor in border areas. The United States and Britain allow pilots to strike any part of the Iraqi air defense system, not just those directly targeting U.S./British aircraft. The result is up to five tons of bombs dropped on Iraq per month with 144 civilians (members of minority groups in the region) killed and 446 injured in 1999 alone. Francis Boyle, professor of international law at University of Illinois College of Law has criticized the bombings. "It is the U.S. government that is violating the U.N. Charter . . . by using military force to allegedly 'police' these illegal 'no-fly' zones that have never been authorized by the U.N. Security Council or by the U.S. Congress, in right of self-defense under U.N. Charter Article 51. The Bush administration has deliberately put U.S. pilots in harm's way in order to concoct a pretext for a catastrophic war of aggression against Iraq. The best way for the American people to protect the lives of our military personnel in the Persian Gulf is to bring them all home." Will the United States continue to enforce these "no fly zones?" Review the "U.S. Government Response Options" and predict how the U.S. government will respond.

U.S. Government Responses on Iraq

SITUATION #1 (1982): IRAN-IRAQ WAR

The Reagan-Bush administration removed Iraq from its list of countries that support terrorism and sold weapons to Iraq, despite heated objections from some members of Congress.

SITUATION #2 (1983): IRAQ USES CHEMICAL WEAPONS AGAINST IRAN

The U.S. State Department news release said, "The United States strongly condemns the prohibited use of chemical weapons wherever it occurs." However the official condemnation was not backed by any action. The state department added that the United States "finds the present Iranian regime's intransigent refusal to deviate from its avowed objective of eliminating the legitimate government of neighboring Iraq to be inconsistent with the accepted norms of behavior among nations." More importantly, the U.S. government:

- restored full diplomatic relations with Iraq.
- allowed U.S. corporations such as Union Carbide and Honeywell to sell supplies to Iraq.
- gave more than $1 billion of loan credits to Iraq.
- gave intelligence information to help Iraq fight Iran.

In private, the United States considered "any major reversal of Iraq's fortunes as a strategic defeat for the West."(National Security Defense Directive 114 and sworn affidavit from former National Security Council official Howard Teicher). Rumsfeld did not criticize Saddam Hussein when he met with him, but only mentioned in passing to the Iraqi foreign minister that Iraq's use of chemical weapons "inhibited" U.S. efforts to assist Iraq.

SITUATION #3 (1988): IRAQ USES BANNED WEAPONS AGAINST THE KURDS

The White House under Ronald Reagan and George H.W. Bush blocked the Senate resolutions for sanctions. Assistant Secretary of State Richard Murphy wrote, "The U.S.-Iraqi relationship is … important to our long-term political and economic objectives. … We believe that economic sanctions will be useless or counterproductive to influence the Iraqis."

Michael Dobbs reported in the *Washington Post* (12/30/03) that Iraqi gassing of the Kurds

> provoked outrage on Capitol Hill and renewed demands for sanctions against Iraq. The State Department and White House were also outraged—but not to the point of doing anything that might seriously damage relations with Baghdad.

Although U.S. arms manufacturers were not as deeply involved as German or British companies in selling weaponry to Iraq, the Reagan administration effectively turned a blind eye to the export of 'dual use' items such as chemical precursors and steel tubes that can have military and civilian applications. In December 1988, Dow Chemical sold Iraq $1.5 million of pesticides that could be used as chemical warfare agents.

SITUATION #4 (JULY 1990): IRAQ THREATENS KUWAIT

According to Iraqi transcripts—there were no official U.S. transcripts of the meeting—the U.S. government maintained the stance that the United States did not have an opinion on Arab-Arab conflicts. Ambassador April Glaspie disputed parts of the Iraqi transcript but admitted that a "great deal" of it was accurate.

However, beyond this one disputed meeting, the United States made no public warnings against Saddam's actions in late July. The United States prepared for war if Iraq invaded. In July, the Pentagon was busy running a computerized military exercise to explore possible responses to "the Iraqi threat" that focused on a hypothetical Iraqi invasion of Kuwait and Saudi Arabia. [William Blum, author of *Killing Hope: U.S. Military and CIA Interventions Since WWII*] At a war games exercise at the Naval War College in Newport, R.I., participants were also being asked to determine the most effective American response to a hypothetical invasion of Kuwait by Iraq.

SITUATION #5 (AUG. 2, 1990): IRAQ INVADES KUWAIT

The U.S. government gave only 48 hours for Arab mediation and agreed to only one brief attempt at negotiation in January 1991 (one week before war). The United States convinced Saudi Arabia to allow U.S. troops to amass more than 200,000 troops on Saudi soil for war against Iraq. In November, Saddam Hussein took hostages to use as "human shields" to ward off attack. Also in November, the United States pushed the U.N. Security Council to pass a resolution demanding that Iraq withdraw unconditionally by Jan. 15 or face a U.N. military action. President George H. W. Bush appealed to the American people: "Our jobs, our way of life, our own freedom and the freedom of friendly countries around the world will suffer if control of the world's great oil reserves fall into the hands of one man, Saddam Hussein."

SITUATION #6 (JAN. 17, 1991): IRAQI WATER AND ELECTRICAL FACILITIES TARGETED

The U.S. military destroyed Iraq's infrastructure. More than 100,000 air missions dropped 88,000 tons of bombs (equivalent to seven and a half Hiroshimas) in 42 days, resulting in an estimated 5,000 to 10,000 immediate civilian deaths and more than 100,000 military fatalities. The Pentagon admitted later that nonmilitary facilities had been extensively targeted for political reasons. A U.S. Air Force planner during the Gulf War said: "Big picture, we wanted to let people know, 'Get rid of this guy and we'll be more than happy to assist in rebuilding. We're not going to tolerate Saddam Hussein or his regime. Fix that, and we'll fix your electricity.'" On February 15, Saddam offered to withdraw from Kuwait and follow all U.N. resolutions, but President Bush rejected his offer as a "cruel hoax."

SITUATION #7 (JANUARY 1991): DEPLETED URANIUM

The United States did use depleted uranium (and used it again in the Iraq war that began in 2003). According to Dr. Helen Caldicott, writing in the *Baltimore Sun*, by the end of the first Gulf War the United States had left between 300 and 800 tons of depleted uranium 238 in antitank shells and other explosives on the battlefields of Iraq, Kuwait, and Saudi Arabia. Of 696,628 U.S. troops who served in the first Gulf War, 183,629 filed for service-related disabilities. It's unknown how many of these may have been caused by exposure to depleted uranium.

Gulf War veteran and anti-depleted uranium activist Dan Fahey explained: "I could go through their [U.S. military] earliest reports on this issue.... This is one from 1990 where they say: 'the most exposed individuals are the soldiers who go to the battlefield after DU rounds are shot,' saying that civilians and soldiers can suffer health effects from the ingestion and inhalation of DU dust, and even saying that once people realize the health and environmental effects of this weapon, there might be a move to ban it. And this is July 1990—this is just six months or so before the war. You have to wonder why no warning was ever disseminated to any ground forces prior to the war."

Paul Sullivan, president of the National Gulf War Veterans Resource Center, reported: "More than 436,000 U.S. troops are confirmed to have entered into those areas of radioactive toxic waste. And sadly, some soldiers camped in areas contaminated by depleted uranium radioactive toxic waste for up to two months without any idea, without any warning at all."

Anuar Abdul Mehsen, an Iraqi doctor who studies cancer, said: "If we compare the mortality rate, that is, the number of patients who die because of cancers, in 1988 we had only 34 patients who died because of cancer. But in 1998 we recorded 428 patients who died because of cancer. Cancers that normally affect elderly people, now they are seen in younger age groups. I have a patient who has cancer of the ovaries who is 11 years old."

SITUATION 8 (MARCH 1991): SHIITE-KURD REBELLION

U.S. and coalition forces stopped the fight against Iraqi forces in southern Iraq and did not go after Saddam in Baghdad. The U.S. also allowed Saddam to use armed helicopters to kill the rebels.

SITUATION #9 (1998): SANCTIONS HURT CIVILIANS

The United States did not push for the removal of sanctions. In fact, the United States led the United Nations in maintaining sanctions. The United States determined what could and could not enter the country. Medicines and chlorine needed to treat drinking water were banned as dual-use chemicals. The United States said that Saddam Hussein's lack of cooperation was the real cause of extending the sanctions and for the suffering of the Iraqi people.

SITUATION #10 (1998-2002): NO-FLY ZONE

The United States and Britain continued the "no-fly zones," saying that it was a strategy to protect the ethnic groups. They blamed Saddam Hussein for locating military equipment near the civilians.

The U.S. and Iraq: Choices and Predictions

DISCUSSION QUESTIONS

Review your predictions and the actual outcomes of each situation and answer the following questions. Use specific details and facts to prove your point.

1. How has U.S. policy on Iraq been consistent or inconsistent?

2. What do you think were the consequences of U.S. policy in Iraq from 1982-1998:
   ▪ on the U.S. role in the world?
   ▪ on civilians in Iraq?
   ▪ on the rest of the world's perception of the United States?

3. Former Assistant Secretary of State Richard Murphy said that "the U.S.-Iraqi relationship is … important to our long-term political and economic objectives." What are U.S. political and economic objectives in the Middle East?

4. Former U.S. Secretary of State Henry Kissinger once said, "Oil is too important a commodity to be left in the hands of the Arabs." What does that reveal about U.S. political and economic objectives?

5. Pick two or three of the choices the U.S. government made and discuss why you agree or disagree with those decisions.

6. Discuss the U.S. decision to use depleted uranium and to bomb water and electrical facilities. Is this a case of the end justifying the means? Is it O.K. to knowingly harm civilians in war?

7. What do you think about Saddam Hussein being given assistance by the United States while he was using weapons of mass destruction? Why do you think that the U.S. government criticized his past use of weapons of mass destruction to justify the 2003 war if they turned a blind eye during the period he was actually using them?

8. How do the U.S. government decisions of the past help you understand the 2003 war?

9. What questions do you have that are raised by the information in this lesson?

Why Invade Iraq?

Analyzing Bush's State of the Union speech

BILL BIGELOW

Materials Needed:

A copy of "President Bush's State of the Union" for each student in the class.

In his State of the Union speech on January 28, 2003, President George W. Bush made his case to the American people for why it might be necessary to go to war against Iraq. "We seek peace," he claimed. "We strive for peace." But a few weeks later he commanded the U.S. military to invade Iraq.

In light of subsequent events, this speech makes for interesting reading—both for what it includes as well as for what it omits. For example, the entire speech focuses on the alleged terrorist threat that Saddam Hussein's Iraq posed to the world. The speech says almost nothing about bringing freedom and democracy to Iraq—which became an alleged war aim only later, as it became increasingly obvious that weapons of mass destruction would not be discovered. Nor is oil mentioned, or any other benefit that American corporations might derive from rebuilding an Iraq integrated into the global capitalist system.

As educators, it's our responsibility to equip students to read critically—especially documents that have potentially lethal consequences. In this activity, the teacher plays George Bush and delivers the Iraq portion of his speech. For the purposes of the lesson, we imagine that the president made himself available for questioning afterwards. Students pepper the teacher-as-president with critical questions and the teacher does his or her best to respond as Bush might have responded. Following the question-and-answer session, the students analyze the speech.

This is an activity that could be used at different points in a study of the Iraq War. Doing this activity before students are knowledgeable about the war will alert them to the Bush administration's rationale for invading Iraq. However, students will be better equipped to think critically about Bush's assertions after they've studied more about the war.

SUGGESTED PROCEDURE:

1. Students should be seated in rows. Tell them that former President George W. Bush is coming to class and will deliver a speech about Iraq and the responsibility of the United States.

2. Distribute copies of "President Bush's State of the Union." Offer a little bit of context for the speech, e.g., this was delivered about two months before the United States invaded; and before the United States abandoned efforts to get the U.N. Security Council to support military action. Instruct students that they should: listen carefully; mark places in the speech that they disagree with, find unclear, or want more details about; and come up with questions to ask the president after the speech.

3. Ask a student to introduce you as the president. This insures that there is a clear point at which you are no longer the teacher, but in your role as President Bush.

4. Read the speech with an appropriate degree of gravity.

5. Hold a press conference, and invite students to raise questions or make critical comments about the speech. Do your best to respond to students' remarks as President Bush might have.

6. After the press conference, ask students to write reviews of the president's speech. Or you could assign them to choose a specific number of points from the speech and to analyze these one by one.

7. The following follow-up questions could be used for writing assignments or class discussion:

▪ What is an "outlaw regime"? If Saddam Hussein's regime was outside the law, what law is Bush referring to?

▪ President Bush says that "we are called to defend the safety of our people and the hopes of all mankind. And once again we accept this responsibility." Who is the "we" that Bush refers to? According to international law, who is entitled to initiate force against other nations?

▪ What evidence of Bush's do you find convincing? What evidence don't you find convincing?

▪ Does the history of U.S.-Iraq relations raise any questions about Bush's speech?

▪ What is Bush's attitude toward the United Nations?

▪ President Bush says that the United States "will prevail." What does it mean to "prevail" in a war with Iraq?

▪ The president says that "freedom is the right of every person and the future of every nation." What kind of freedom is Bush talking about? Is this standard of freedom applied to all U.S. allies—for example, to Saudi Arabia?

▪ Can you find any inaccuracies in Bush's speech? [For example, the claim that Iraq sought to buy "significant quantities of uranium from Africa" was false. The bipartisan commission investigating the events of September 11 found no evidence that Iraq had ties with al Qaeda. U.S. forces and subsequent inspections found no weapons of mass destruction.]

▪ The president speaks of war being "forced upon us." Do you believe that war was forced upon us? What evidence supports your opinion? Also, consider Bush's use of the word "us." In what way is this "our" war? In what way is it not "our" war?

▪ Do subsequent events in Iraq raise any further questions about the State of the Union address? ▪

State of the Union Address

THE FOLLOWING ARE EXCERPTS FROM PRESIDENT BUSH'S STATE OF THE UNION ADDRESS, JANUARY 28, 2003:

Today, the gravest danger in the war on terror, the gravest danger facing America and the world, is outlaw regimes that seek and possess nuclear, chemical, and biological weapons. These regimes could use such weapons for blackmail, terror, and mass murder. They could also give or sell those weapons to terrorist allies, who would use them without the least hesitation.

This threat is new; America's duty is familiar. Throughout the 20th century, small groups of men seized control of great nations, built armies and arsenals, and set out to dominate the weak and intimidate the world. In each case, their ambitions of cruelty and murder had no limit. In each case, the ambitions of Hitlerism, militarism, and communism were defeated by the will of free peoples, by the strength of great alliances, and by the might of the United States of America.

Now, in this century, the ideology of power and domination has appeared again, and seeks to gain the ultimate weapons of terror. Once again, this nation and all our friends are all that stand between a world at peace, and a world of chaos and constant alarm. Once again, we are called to defend the safety of our people, and the hopes of all mankind. And we accept this responsibility.

Twelve years ago, Saddam Hussein faced the prospect of being the last casualty in a war he had started and lost. To spare himself, he agreed to disarm all weapons of mass destruction. For the next 12 years, he systematically violated that agreement. He pursued chemical, biological, and nuclear weapons, even while inspectors were in his country. Nothing to date has restrained him from his pursuit of these weapons—not economic sanctions, not isolation from the civilized world, not even cruise missile strikes on his military facilities.

Almost three months ago, the United Nations Security Council gave Saddam Hussein his final chance to disarm. He has shown instead utter contempt for the United Nations, and for the opinion of the world. The 108 U.N. inspectors were not sent to conduct a scavenger hunt for hidden materials across a country the size of California. The job of the inspectors is to verify that Iraq's regime is disarming. It is up to Iraq to show exactly where it is hiding its banned weapons, lay those weapons out for the world to see, and destroy them as directed. Nothing like this has happened.

The United Nations concluded in 1999 that Saddam Hussein had biological weapons sufficient to produce over 25,000 liters of anthrax—enough doses to kill several million people. He hasn't accounted for that material. He's given no evidence that he has destroyed it.

The United Nations concluded that Saddam Hussein had materials sufficient to produce more than 38,000 liters of botulinum toxin—enough to subject millions of people to death by respiratory failure. He hadn't accounted for that material. He's given no evidence that he has destroyed it.

Our intelligence officials estimate that Saddam Hussein had the materials to produce as much as 500 tons of sarin, mustard, and VX nerve agent. In such quantities, these chemical agents could also kill untold thousands. He's not accounted for these materials. He has given no evidence that he has destroyed them.

U.S. intelligence indicates that Saddam Hussein had upwards of 30,000 munitions capable of delivering chemical agents. Inspectors recently turned up 16 of them—despite Iraq's recent declaration denying their existence. Saddam Hussein has not accounted for the remaining 29,984 of these prohibited munitions. He's given no evidence that he has destroyed them.

From three Iraqi defectors we know that Iraq, in the late 1990s, had several mobile biological weapons labs. These are designed to produce germ warfare agents, and can be moved from place to a place to evade inspectors. Saddam Hussein has not disclosed these facilities. He's given no evidence that he has destroyed them.

The International Atomic Energy Agency confirmed in the 1990s that Saddam Hussein had an advanced nuclear weapons development program, had a design for a nuclear weapon and was working on five different methods of enriching uranium for a bomb. The British government has learned that Saddam Hussein recently sought significant quantities of uranium from Africa. Our intelligence sources tell us that he has attempted to purchase high-strength aluminum tubes suitable for nuclear weapons production. Saddam Hussein has not credibly explained these activities. He clearly has much to hide.

The dictator of Iraq is not disarming. To the contrary; he is deceiving. From intelligence sources we know, for instance, that thousands of Iraqi security personnel are at work hiding documents and materials from the U.N. inspectors, sanitizing inspection sites, and monitoring the inspectors themselves. Iraqi officials accompany the inspectors in order to intimidate witnesses....

Year after year, Saddam Hussein has gone to elaborate lengths, spent enormous sums, taken great risks to build and keep weapons of mass destruction. But why? The only possible explanation, the only possible use he could have for those weapons, is to dominate, intimidate, or attack.

With nuclear arms or a full arsenal of chemical and biological weapons, Saddam Hussein could resume his ambitions of conquest in the Middle East and create deadly havoc in that region. And this Congress and the America people must recognize another threat. Evidence from intelligence sources, secret communications, and statements by people now in custody reveal that Saddam Hussein aids and protects terrorists, including members of al Qaeda. Secretly, and without fingerprints, he could provide one of his hidden weapons to terrorists, or help them develop their own.

Before September the 11th, many in the world believed that Saddam Hussein could be contained. But chemical agents, lethal viruses, and shadowy terrorist networks are not easily contained. Imagine those 19 hijackers with other weapons and other plans—this time armed by Saddam Hussein. It would take one vial, one canister, one crate slipped into this country to bring a day of horror like none we have ever known. We will do everything in our power to make sure that that day never comes.

Some have said we must not act until the threat is imminent. Since when have terrorists and tyrants announced their intentions, politely putting us on notice before they strike? If this threat is permitted to fully and suddenly emerge, all actions, all words, and all recriminations would come too late. Trusting in the sanity and restraint of Saddam Hussein is not a strategy, and it is not an option.

The dictator who is assembling the world's most dangerous weapons has already used them on whole villages—leaving thousands of his own citizens dead, blind, or disfigured. Iraqi refugees tell us how forced confessions are obtained—by torturing children while their parents are made to watch. International human rights groups have catalogued other methods used in the torture chambers of Iraq: electric shock, burning with hot irons, dripping acid on the skin, mutilation with electric drills, cutting out tongues, and rape. If this is not evil, then evil has no meaning.

And tonight I have a message for the brave and oppressed people of Iraq: Your enemy is not surrounding your country—your enemy is ruling your country. And the day he and his regime are removed from power will be the day of your liberation.

The world has waited 12 years for Iraq to disarm. America will not accept a serious and mounting threat to our country, and our friends and our allies. The United States will ask the U.N. Security Council to convene on February the 5th to consider the facts of Iraq's ongoing defiance of the world. Secretary of State Powell will present information and intelligence about Iraq's illegal weapons programs, its attempt to hide those weapons from inspectors, and its links to terrorist groups.

We will consult. But let there be no misunderstanding: If Saddam Hussein does not fully disarm, for the safety of our people and for the peace of the world, we will lead a coalition to disarm him....

Sending Americans into battle is the most profound decision a president can make. The technologies of war have changed; the risks and suffering of war have not. For the brave Americans who bear the risk, no victory is free from sorrow. This nation fights reluctantly, because we know the cost and we dread the days of mourning that always come.

We seek peace. We strive for peace. And sometimes peace must be defended. A future lived at the mercy of terrible threats is no peace at all. If war is forced upon us, we will fight in a just cause and by just means—sparing, in every way we can, the innocent. And if war is forced upon us, we will fight with the full force and might of the United States military—and we will prevail.

And as we and our coalition partners are doing in Afghanistan, we will bring to the Iraqi people food and medicines and supplies—and freedom....

Americans are a free people, who know that freedom is the right of every person and the future of every nation. The liberty we prize is not America's gift to the world, it is God's gift to humanity.

We Americans have faith in ourselves, but not in ourselves alone. We do not know—we do not claim to know all the ways of Providence, yet we can trust in them, placing our confidence in the loving God behind all of life, and all of history.

May He guide us now. And may God continue to bless the United States of America. ▪

$265,000,000
+2,453
"occupation"
COST OF WAR $281,864,94
$0,000
35,161
00,000
3,000,000,000,

MICHAEL DUFFY

The War in Iraq and Daily Classroom Life

Suggestions from a 5th-grade teacher on bringing the war in Iraq into the curriculum

BOB PETERSON
RETHINKING SCHOOLS (Spring 2007)

"That's six PS3s every second!" Juan exclaimed, almost drooling at the thought of putting his hands on Sony's new Playstation video game system. "That's one heck of a lot of money."

The comment came during a mini-math lesson on the cost of the Iraq War that included rather tedious calculations by my entire 5th-grade class. My students had figured out that the United States was spending a little more than $3,000 each second on the war.

The lesson was not part of a major unit on the Iraq War. In fact, not since the beginning of the war in March 2003 have I done such a unit. Since then I have touched on the subject in current events, but like many teachers I find my school day crammed by special projects and the pressures of "covering" the curriculum.

My somewhat nonchalant attitude toward teaching about the war changed abruptly last year during a literature circle discussion with half a dozen children about the book *Number the Stars* by Lois Lowry. The students were discussing the word "occupation," detailing what it meant for the Nazis to rule Holland, the setting of Lowry's novel. Hoping to make the word even more meaningful, I added that some people use the word "occupation" to describe the U.S. military's relation to Iraq.

The students stared at me with blank eyes.

"You know, whether you agree or disagree with it, the U.S. Army and Marines are basically running Iraq," I explained. "I am not comparing the U.S. military to the Nazis, but the word occupation applies to lots of different situations."

Finally, a response.

"You mean that war is still going on?" replied Shaneekwa. "I thought it was over."

"YOU MEAN THAT WAR IS STILL GOING ON?" REPLIED SHANEEKWA. "I THOUGHT IT WAS OVER."

Her comment reminded me that for many Americans, the war is little more than a minor annoyance on the edge of their consciousness. It also made me think about my responsibility as a teacher in a country that spends hundreds of billions of dollars on a war many people around the world think is illegal and immoral. I hadn't intended to ignore the topic with my students, but I had.

Shaneekwa's comment was a wake-up call. It pushed me to find ways to weave the topic of the war—and other important issues such as genocide in Darfur—more actively into my curriculum.

Last spring, for instance, I used statistics from the war in a unit on place value, data, graphing, and large numbers. As one of my "songs of the week," I played Pink's "Dear Mr. President" and we discussed the controversy following a Florida principal's decision not to allow a 4th grader to sing that song in a school talent show. In the song Pink poses questions about homelessness, poverty, and the war, asking, "How do you dream when a mother has no chance to say goodbye?" Following the discussion, Osvaldo, a student who had recently immigrated from Mexico, wrote his own poem to the President using data from the website www.costofwar.com.

"I HAD TO DO SOMETHING"

When the current school year started, I intended to continue discussions of the war with my new class of 5th graders at La Escuela Fratney, an inner-city bilingual school that is predominantly Latino but also has whites and African Americans. We did some Middle East geography and discussed a couple of news stories. But other curricular issues started asserting themselves and, once again, the war became a very minor focus in my classroom.

Over winter break, however, with time to think about my curriculum and with media reports predicting that soon the 3000th U.S. soldier would be killed, I once again decided I could not ignore the issue. I felt guilty realizing my renewed interest was sparked by the deaths of U.S. soldiers—not the tens of thousands of Iraqis who have died. Regardless, I decided I had to do something.

On the first day after vacation I wrote the number "3,000" on the board and asked if anyone knew its significance. "It's a lot," ventured one student, but there was not much more. After I gave a hint that the number had "something to do with what's going on in the world," John raised his hand and said he thought it was the number of soldiers killed in Iraq. After clarifying that it was the number of U.S. soldiers, I asked for comments or questions. One student wanted to know how many Iraqi soldiers had been killed. Another asked how many had been hurt. We also defined "civilian"—a word none of them was familiar with.

One of my students started going off on the "stupid war" and said some derogatory comments about Bush. I made clear that name-calling—even of a political figure you disagree with—is not allowed in my classroom. I also stressed that students were welcome to discuss different points of view.

A normally quiet child then raised her hand and shared that her cousin was in the military. Another boy said that his sister was in Afghanistan. At one point I asked if anyone had family or close friends in the military, and a third of the 25 students raised their hands.

When one student said he thought it was silly to spend so much money on the war, I suggested that we look at a website that tallies the cost of the war. Any mention of the internet sparks interest in my class, so the students all focused on one of our classroom computers, where we went to www.costofwar.com.

The website has a running total of the war's cost, based on congressional appropriations, and the number is constantly increasing. Students were mesmerized as they watched the numbers stream quickly by. After showing them how to freeze the tally, I chose a "good" math student to read the number. As he did so digit by digit, he stumbled and I knew we had to work on understanding and reading large numbers.

I wrote the number on the board and as a class we practiced reading it. In the process, I reviewed place values up to the hundred billions place.

The following day I brought in a newspaper photo of a local "die-in" the previous night, in which antiwar protesters lay on the steps of the federal building. I told the students I had participated, although some were skeptical because I was not part of the photo. We checked the costofwar website again and practiced reading the ever-increasing number.

On the third day, for our early morning activity I had students figure out how much money had been spent in the last three days. Then, by doing a long division problem, we figured out that the United States spends about $265,000,000 per day on the Iraq War. We checked out other parts of the costofwar site and found, for example, that the amount spent on the war thus far is equivalent to 14 million four-year college scholarships. "That's a lot!" exclaimed several students, but the number was so large that it was essentially meaningless to my students.

I tried to make the large numbers more understandable. In one mini-lesson I put dollar bills down on a desk one second at a time and asked how long it would take us to get up to a billion. We figured it would take about 32 years.

In another lesson, I had students figure out the cost of the war using smaller units of time. Working in pairs and then as a large group, and with a whole lot of discussion, we figured out how much of our tax dollars is being spent on the war in an hour, a minute and then a second.

That's when Juan shouted out the number of PS3s that could be bought each second—assuming, Juan clarified, "you buy the $500, not the $600 model." Peter suggested that you could take those six and resell them on e-Bay and make a lot more money.

Numbers Count
Numbers do count Mr. President
2,453 America soldiers are dying
17,648 soldiers are wounded
35,161 innocent Iraqi people are dying
281,864,948,707 dollars
are wasted in the war.
Imagine how much we can do around the world
With that money!
We can feed the needy
Build houses
Give scholarships
And much more
Do you care about the people?
I do.
—Osvaldo
 5th grade, La Escuela Fratney,
May 2006

Message Poem to George W. Bush
Bush sends troops
Day and night
Soldiers come
To a never ending fight
Killing many, hurting families
Not even realizing what he's done
He spent billions of dollars on a war
He thinks of himself and not others
Selfish I call him
He doesn't care
No matter how much we vote
He acts as if we're not there
To me he's a fool
He could've used that money
To put children in school.
—Gianna
 5th grade
 La Escuela Fratney

My attempt at getting kids to reflect on the social cost of the war was losing out to their entrepreneurial spirit and their obsessive fascination with the latest video game technology. My frown must have communicated my disappointment because Juan quickly added that with all that extra money from the e-Bay sales, "We'd have all the more money to help people who needed it."

I made one last attempt to concretize the cost by having a student go to the costofwar website section on public education. It shows that the nearly $350 billion spent on the war thus far could have been used to hire six million teachers for one year. I told the kids that given there are about 80,000 public schools in the United States, every school could have 75 more teachers—or each school could get two more teachers for the next 38 years. Given that we don't have a music or gym teacher in our school, students related to that.

"No offense, Mr. Bob," one told me later. "You're a good gym teacher, we'd just like to have a real one."

I didn't want class discussions to focus primarily on math, however, or on my merits as a gym teacher. I wanted students to explore what they thought, not only about the war but other pressing social issues. I encouraged them to write their feelings and thoughts in their journal or as part of a bilingual poetry book that each is expected to complete. I shared a few poems that former students had written on the war and other social topics, including Osvaldo's from the year before, and suggested that my students might write a "message" poem on a topic they felt strongly about.

The various mini-lessons had an impact and over time, the war became an ongoing topic of conversation, albeit at a low level. For example, a student might announce the new cost of the war, based on an internet search they have done the night before. A few wear peace buttons they have gotten from other family members.

Many of my students' families, including those who have members in the military, have become increasingly critical of the war. This has posed the dilemma of how to make sure that articulate, outspoken critics of the war don't dominate class discussions. I also want to make sure that students, regardless of their view, base their perspectives on sound facts and reasoning. As a result, I challenge statements, even those I may agree with, if they are merely asserted and not backed up. I want my students to learn to think and form their own opinions.

MOVING TO ACTION

For a number of my students, the most significant lesson came outside the classroom.

When I talked about the "die-in" I participated in, some students wanted to know when the next protest would be. I told them there would be a march in Washington on Jan. 27, and several suggested we organize a class field trip to the march. I declined. (One student did make the trip with his father, travelling 14 hours each way.)

I also noted there was going to be a local peace rally the same weekend and that I knew some of the organizers, who had previously told me they would be interested in students speaking at the rally. I told this to my class and several students expressed interest. With their parents' permission, over the next two weeks several students stayed in during recess to write speeches and make signs.

Three students—two of whom have relatives in the military—spoke at the protest, with the full support and participation of their parents and families. A few other students and their families attended as well. The three student speakers were warmly received by the more than 100 people at the rally, which was attended mainly by veterans and was held inside Milwaukee's City Hall Rotunda on a cold Friday evening.

Gabriela was the first of my students to speak, and began by saying, "I believe the Iraq war is the most unnecessary war the United States has ever been in." She paused, as I had suggested in our rehearsals, and the thunderous applause gave her the courage to make an impassioned plea for peace.

When she was done, Gabriela introduced Malachi, whose sister was returning the next day from a tour of duty in Afghanistan. He read a poem he had written:

Dear Mr. President please stop this war.

My sister's in the military and we don't understand what this war is for.

It's hard, cold and mean.

No more war for oil schemes

I don't want her to go

I love her so.

3,000 dead

46,000 injured

What's the point?

10's of thousands of Iraqis dead

Bring them home

Don't send countless more

Mr. President, Please, Please, Please

Stop this war.

The third student speaker was Riscardo, who has several relatives in the armed forces. He noted that he thought some wars, such as the War of Independence and World War II's defeat of Hitler, "are okay and necessary." But, he continued, "some wars are suicidal, like the Vietnam War and the Iraq War."

Riscardo ended his speech by saying, "There are billions of dollars being spent and thousands of soldiers and civilians are dying, so we have to make sure to stop this war. End the Iraq War!"

It's a refrain that is increasingly common across the United States. And yet the war continues. Until it ends, I have a responsibility to see that it is discussed and studied in my classroom. ■

Bob Peterson (repmilw@aol.com) is an editor of Rethinking Schools. On September 9, 2004, at the Smithsonian National Museum of American History in Washington, Dickinson College honored Peterson for his innovative approaches to teaching about 9/11. He is currently the president of the Milwaukee Teachers' Education Association.

Except for the students who spoke at the public rally and the authors of the poems, the names have been changed.

CHAPTER 3

The Human Face of War

Save the Muslim Girl

Looking critically at popular YA fiction set in Muslim cultures

ÖZLEM SENSOY AND ELIZABETH MARSHALL
***RETHINKING SCHOOLS* (Winter 2009)**

Young adult titles that focus on the lives of Muslim girls in the Middle East, written predominantly by white women, have appeared in increasing numbers since Sept. 11, 2001. A short list includes Deborah Ellis's trilogy *The Breadwinner*, *Parvana's Journey*, and *Mud City*; Suzanne Fisher Staples' *Under the Persimmon Tree*; and, more recently, Kim Antieau's *Broken Moon*. These titles received high praise and starred reviews from publications like *Horn Book* and *Publishers Weekly*. Each features a young heroine trapped in a violent Middle East from which she must escape or save herself, her family, and other innocents in the region. Authors portray Muslim girls overwhelmingly as characters haunted by a sad past, on the cusp of a (usually arranged) marriage, or impoverished and wishing for the freedoms that are often assigned to the West, such as education, safety, and prosperity.

Young adult literature about the Middle East cannot be separated from the post-9/11 context in which these books are marketed and increasingly published. Deborah Ellis' *The Breadwinner*, for instance, was originally published in 2000, but Groundwood publishers rushed to re-release a paperback reprint of it in the United States after 9/11 (Roback & Britton, 2001). Since that time it has been translated into 17 languages and has become an international bestseller (Atkinson, 2003); in 2004 it was selling an estimated 15,000 copies a month in the United States (Baker & Atkinson, 2004). "Save the Muslim girl" stories emerge alongside a preoccupation with Islam in mainstream news media and a surge in U.S. and Canadian military, political, and economic activities in the Middle East and West Asia. The texts are framed and packaged to sell in a marketplace at a particular moment when military interventions are centered on Afghanistan and other predominantly Muslim countries.

> THESE YOUNG ADULT NOVELS SERVE AS DE-FACTO LEGITIMIZATION FOR THE U.S.-LED INCURSIONS IN THE REGION AS A PROJECT OF WOMEN'S EMANCIPATION.

As many teachers have found, these stories offer an enticing way for students to engage with current events, language arts, and social studies curricula. However, given that these books are written for and marketed primarily to a Western audience, what ideas do they teach young adult readers about Muslim girls, Islam, and the Middle East? In what follows, we detail three lessons that dominate the "save the Muslim girl" stories.

Our interest here is not to defend any particular doctrine (fundamentalist Christian or Islamic). Rather, in this article we identify how these books reproduce—and offer opportunities to challenge—longstanding ideas commonly associated with Islam: backwardness, oppression, and cultural decay. We believe that these novels can best be used to teach about the common Western stereotypes that are universalized in these books rather than to teach about Afghanistan, Pakistan, or Islamic cultures.

LEARNING A STEREOTYPE, LESSON #1:
Muslim Girls Are Veiled, Nameless, and Silent

Young adult books about the Muslim girl usually feature a veiled adolescent on the cover. Her face is cropped and concealed, usually by her own hands or her veil. Much of her face is covered, including, most significantly, her mouth. Images serve as a shorthand vocabulary. Consider how iconic images—a white or black cowboy hat, a scientist wearing a white lab coat, a princess—set up a stock plot. The repeated images of veiled girls reinforce familiar, mainstream ideas about the confined existence of Muslim women and girls. This is the Muslim girl story we expect to read.

These kinds of images have a long history in the West. Steve McCurry's famous 1985 photo of 13-year-old Sharbat Gula on the cover of National Geographic provides the most well-known example. When we show the photo of the famous green-eyed Afghani girl in our education courses and ask students to write what they know about her, every student recognizes her image, yet few if any know her name, where she comes from, or that her photograph was "captured" in a refugee camp by a white U.S. journalist. Interestingly, the 2004 Oxford edition of Deborah Ellis's *Mud City* reproduces a photo of Sharbat Gula on its front cover, taken from the same series of photographs McCurry captured in the mid-1980s (see Figure 1). The cover of Antieau's *Broken Moon* has a virtually identical image: a close shot of a young girl with a veil covering her mouth, and her hands cupping her lower face (see Figure 2). What ideas about Muslim or Middle Eastern girls—specifically Afghani girls—are we as audience invited to imagine?

Just about every book in this genre features such an image on its cover. These are familiar metaphors for how the Muslim girl's life will be presented within the novel. The way the girls' mouths are covered reinforces existing ideas about their silence and suggests that we in the West (conceptualized as "free" and "liberated") need to help unveil and "give" them voice. The images also invite ideas about girlhood innocence and vulnerability, and invite Western readers to protect, save, and speak for these oppressed girls.

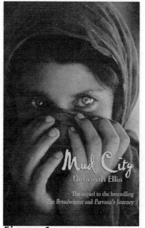

Figure 1   Figure 2

But, is it not true that Muslim girls are oppressed and voiceless? We would argue that all women experience gender discrimination in different ways and with different consequences. The experiences of a U.S. woman (for example) will vary greatly if she is heterosexual or a lesbian, living in an urban center or a rural area.

Imagine this rural lesbian is black, or black and Muslim, or black, Muslim, and a non-native English speaker. In this way, her experiences are determined not simply by her gender, but also by her racial, ethnic, and sexual identity. What strikes us about the books that we review here is that they are written by white Western women who author, organize, and interpret stories about Middle Eastern girlhoods for Western consumption. This raises questions about the politics of storytelling. For instance, how do (white) Western women decide for "global" women what their issues and oppressions are? Who tells whose story and in what ways?

Richard Dyer reminds us that while we may believe that stereotypes are derived from a limited truth about particular people, we actually get our ideas about people from stereotypic images. So it isn't the kernel of truth that results in stereotypes. Stereotypes are created and reinforced by the repeated appearance of particular images and the exclusion of others. Thus, the repeated circulation of the image of the veiled, sad Muslim girl reinforces the stereotype that all Muslim girls are oppressed.

Stereotypes are particularly powerful in the case of groups with which one has little or no personal relationship. Thus, for young people who get most of their ideas about "others" from textbooks or from media, we need to ask what ideas are learned when they "see" a very limited image of Muslim girls.

LEARNING A STEREOTYPE, LESSON #2:
Veiled = Oppressed

Gendered violence in Middle Eastern countries, or the threat of it, organizes many of the books' plots. With few exceptions, the "good" civilized men in the girl's family are taken from her. In *Under the Persimmon Tree*, a brother and father are forced to join the Taliban as fighters, while in *The Breadwinner*, the Taliban places the father in jail because he was educated in England. *Parvana's Journey* opens with the father's funeral, and a deceased dad also figures in *Broken Moon*. This absence leaves the heroine vulnerable to the roving, indiscriminate, uncivilized "bad" men who will beat her for going out without a male escort (*The Breadwinner* and *Broken Moon*), confine her to the house (*The Breadwinner*), or beat her to preserve the honor of the community (*Broken Moon*).

In this context of an absent/immobilized parent, the girl is placed at the center of the plot, further emphasizing the danger and vulnerability of her existence. Parvana in *The Breadwinner* and *Parvana's Journey*, Nadira in *Broken Moon*, and Najmah in *Under the Persimmon Tree* each cut their hair and disguise themselves as boys. This cross-dressing draws heavily on Western ideas that girls should be unfettered by the requirement to cover themselves, and authors present this type of transformation as the only humane alternative to wearing a burqa and the only way to travel safely outside the domestic sphere.

The veil or burqa, which has exclusively functioned as the short-hand marker of women's oppression, is a much more complicated thing. To give you a sense of the range of meaning of the veil, consider for instance that in Turkey—a predominantly Muslim country—the veil (or "religious dress") is outlawed in public spaces as a means to underline the government's commitments to Kemalism, a "modern," secularist stance. In response and as a sign of resistance, some women, especially young university students and those in urban areas, consider the veil to be a marker of protest against government regulation of their bodies and the artificial division of "modern" versus "faithful." Similar acts of resistance are taken up by feminists in Egypt who wear the veil as a conscious act of resistance against Western imperialism. As another example, before 9/11, the Revolutionary Association of Women in Afghanistan (RAWA) documented the Taliban's crimes against girls and women by hiding video cameras under their burqas and transformed the burqa from simply a marker of oppression to a tool of resistance.

It is problematic to wholly and simplistically equate women's oppression with the burqa, just as it would be problematic to claim that once Western women stop using make-up to cover their faces, it will mean an end to domestic violence in the United States and Canada. While veiling has different meanings in different contexts, it exclusively carries a negative connotation in the "save the Muslim girl" texts. For example, in *The Breadwinner*, the reader is educated about the burqa

> **IT IS PROBLEMATIC TO SIMPLISTICALLY EQUATE WOMEN'S OPPRESSION WITH THE BURQA.**

through the main character, Parvana:

"How do women in burqas manage to walk along the streets?" Parvana asked her father. "How do they see where they are going?"

"They fall down a lot," her father replied.

Nusrat, the American aid worker in Staples's *Under the Persimmon Tree*, describes the burqa similarly: "In the cool autumn air, Nusrat forgets how suffocating the folds of the burqa's synthetic fabric can be in hot weather, and how peering through the crocheted latticework eye piece can feel like looking through the bars of a prison."

In contrast to these confined women, the heroines of these novels, like "free" girls in the West, wear pants and experience freedom of movement. The freedoms associated with Western women are further emphasized in these texts by the addition of non-Muslim characters. The French nurse in *Parvana's Journey* (who works in Pakistan for a relief agency) and the American Nusrat in *Under the Persimmon Tree* (who establishes and runs a school for refugees) each choose to come to the Middle East to help. A white woman veterinarian who "wore the clothes of a Westerner" tends to the camels in *Broken Moon*. These "choices" that enable non-Muslim women to move and to work are placed in contrast to the experiences of the girls/women in the story who are at the mercy of violent events and settings in which their mobility (not to mention their way of dress) is strictly regulated and supervised.

There is a compelling character in *The Breadwinner* who offers the potential to represent Afghani women's liberation in more complex ways. This is Mrs. Weera, who leads a women's resistance group. She also convinces Parvana's mother to join her in running a covert school for girls. It is regrettable that Mrs. Weera does not occupy a more central place in the story since, unlike any other adult woman in the "save the Muslim girl" literature, she offers a transformative representation of activism among Muslim women in Afghanistan.

Again, we want to reiterate that we are not arguing that women and girls in the Middle East or predominantly Islamic societies do not experience domestic violence. In fact, we believe that domestic violence is a global epidemic that most countries, including predominantly Christian countries such as Canada and the United States, have neglected to face head on. Rather, we are arguing that the victim narrative that is so often a part of these young adult novels about Middle Eastern women reinforces the idea that the region is inherently violent and that women must be protected by outside forces. These young adult novels serve as de-facto legitimization for the U.S.-led incursions in the region as a project of women's emancipation. As Laura Bush argued in her radio address on Nov. 17, 2001: "The brutal oppression of women is a central goal of the terrorists." In this way, the complexities of Afghanistan's history, as well as U.S. interest in the region and ties to violence, escape attention.

That girls in the Middle East are consistently at risk of gendered violence implicitly suggests that girls in the "civilized" West are immune to such threats. The education students with whom we work are very familiar and comfortable with the stereotype that the lives of Muslim women are inherently scary, that they cannot work or vote or walk around without the threat of violence. Of course there are Muslim women who live in oppressive or patriarchal regimes (in the Middle East and elsewhere). What we contend is that young adult novels written by white women and marketed and consumed in the West consistently reinforce the idea that Muslim women are inherently oppressed, that they are oppressed in ways that Western women are not, and that this oppression is a function of Islam. By positioning "Eastern" women as the women who are truly oppressed, those in the West pass up a rich opportunity to engage in complex questions about oppression, patriarchy, war, families, displacement, and the role of values (imperialist or faith-based) in these relations.

While some might argue that an author's literary imagination is her own, we suggest that these representations of Muslim girls do not—and cannot—exist independent of a social context. That these "save the Muslim girl" stories continue to be marketed by major publishers, reviewed favorably by literary and educational gatekeepers, and/or achieve bestseller status like *The Breadwinner* suggests an intimate connection to the current ideological climate within which these stories are told, marketed, and consumed.

LEARNING A STEREOTYPE, LESSON #3:
Muslim Girls and Women Want To Be Saved by the West

For many in the West, the plight of Afghanistan is framed exclusively within a post 9/11, U.S.-led "war on terror." While radical women's organizations like RAWA have condemned brutality against women in Afghanistan for decades, their voices were absent, and are now muted, in a landscape of storytelling that is dominated by white Western women representing them. In an open letter to Ms. magazine, for instance, a U.S.-based supporter of RAWA notes that U.S.-centric women's organizations such as the Feminist Majority fail to give "credit to the independent Afghan women who stayed in Afghanistan and Pakistan throughout the 23-year (and counting) crisis in Afghanistan and provided relief, education, resistance and hope to the women and men of their country." Novels like Broken Moon play on popular scripts in which the West saves the people of the "East." These stories cannot be seen as simply works of fiction. They ultimately influence real world experiences of girls in the Middle East and (most relevant to us) of Muslim and non-Muslim girls in our schools in the West.

Deborah Ellis and Suzanne Fisher Staples gain legitimacy as authors because they have visited, lived, and/or spoken to real girls and women in the Middle East. *The Breadwinner* trilogy and *Under the Persimmon Tree* each include a map and an author's note that touches on the "tumultuous" history of Afghanistan and a glossary. The history offered in the end matter and in the texts themselves glosses over the history of colonization in the region. The authors dilute what is an extremely complex history that has led up to the current violence in the Middle East, particularly the role of U.S. foreign policy and military interventions that contributed to the rise of the Taliban.

The authors fail to capture the complexities of U.S. involvement and intervention in favor of stereotypical lessons about educating and saving Muslim girls. As Sonali Kolhatkar, vice president of the Afghan Women's Mission, and Mariam Rawi, a member of the Revolutionary Association of the Women of Afghanistan (RAWA), argue: "Feminists and other humanitarians should learn from history. This isn't the first time the welfare of women has been trotted out as a pretext for imperialist military aggression." (2009) On one level these texts are part of a larger public pedagogy in which the United States and its allies are framed as fighting a good fight in Afghanistan and other regions of the Middle East. Readers are encouraged to continue to empathize with the lead character and the ideas that are associated with her: saving wounded children rather than critiquing U.S. policy, "pulling oneself up by one's bootstraps" rather than organizing together, fighting against all odds—ideas firmly rooted in mainstream U.S. ideals of exceptionalism and Western values of individuality.

TEACHING A MORE COMPLICATED TRUTH

We support teachers using books like *The Breadwinner* with the pedagogical goals of critical examination. We are not advocating for the one "right" Muslim girl story, nor do we suggest that teachers avoid using these books in classrooms (for we recognize that in many cases, decisions about what books teachers have access to are made by economic constraints at the school and district levels). We would, however, like to offer suggestions for the kinds of questions teachers could ask in order to use these resources in ways that are critically minded:

- How are Muslim girls visually depicted on the cover? You might ask students to generate a list of adjectives that describe the girl. The curriculum Scarves of Many Colors is a terrific resource for exploring the relationship between graphics and students' ideas about people. Consider questions of accuracy, context, and motivation. For example: How accurate are the details in the image? When and how will this image be "made sense of"? Who produced this image and why?
- Which parts of the novel are you absolutely certain are true? How do you know? Where did you learn this information? Students can try to pinpoint the resources they rely upon to get their "facts."

- Who is the author of this story? How do they legitimize themselves as an expert? What might be their motivations? Who are they speaking to and for?
- How is the book marketed and what does it intend to teach Western readers? Students might examine the description on the back of the book, the author's note, the map, the glossary, and book reviews to make observations about what kinds of readers are being targeted.
- How does Afghanistan (or Pakistan) fit into the region? In the author's note, Deborah Ellis points out that Afghanistan has been at war for decades. Often we study one country at a time. A more critical approach would investigate the relationships among countries. Students could explore the historical and current relationships (economic, political, cultural) between Afghanistan and other nation-states such as the former Soviet Union, Pakistan, Iran, and China.
- Whose story is missing? Students can create visual representations of the social locations (e.g., the race, class, gender, education) of each of the characters. Given these details, whose story is this? Whose stories are not here, and where might we go to learn about their stories?

While these examples of young adult fictions do not offer much in the way of transformative education about the Middle East, they do offer the potential to educate us about our own assumptions and our pedagogical purposes when we teach the "oppressed Muslim girl" stories. It is in this capacity that we hope educators will take up these novels. ▪

Özlem Sensoy teaches in the Faculty of Education at Simon Fraser University in Canada. She recently published Muslim Voices in School: Narratives of Identity and Pluralism. *Elizabeth Marshall, a former elementary school teacher, teaches courses on children's and young adult literature at Simon Fraser University. This article originally appeared in the Winter 2009-10 issue of* Rethinking Schools.

References

Antieau, Kim. *Broken Moon*. New York: Margaret K. McElderry Books, 2007.

Bigelow, Bill, Sandra Childs, Norm Diamond, Diana Dickerson, and Jan Haaken. *Scarves of Many Colors: Muslim Women and the Veil*. Washington, D.C.: Teaching for Change, 2000.

Dyer, Richard. *The Matter of Images: Essays on Representation*. New York: Routledge, 1993.

Ellis, Deborah. *The Breadwinner*. Toronto: Groundwood Books, 2000.

Ellis, Deborah. *Parvana's Journey*. Toronto: Groundwood Books, 2002.

Ellis, Deborah. *Mud City*. Toronto: Groundwood Books, 2003.

Kolhatkar, Sonali & Rawi, Mariam. "Why Is a Leading Feminist Organization Lending Its Name to Support Escalation in Afghanistan?" July 8, 2009: www.alternet.org/world/141165.

Miller, Elizabeth. "An Open Letter to the Editors of Ms. Magazine." *Off Our Backs*. September/March 2002: 59-61.

Sensoy, Özlem. "Ickity Ackity Open Sesame: Learning About the Middle East in Images." *Rethinking Curricular Knowledge on Global Societies*. Ed. Binaya Subedi. Charlotte, N.C.: Information Age Publishing, 2009: 39-55.

Staples, Suzanne Fisher. *Under the Persimmon Tree*. New York: Simon & Schuster, 2005.

Baghdad Burning Heats Up World History

Young Iraqi woman's blog gives students a window on the civilian experience of war

JODY SOKOLOWER
RETHINKING SCHOOLS (Winter 2009)

The trouble with world history is it started so long ago," I complained to anyone who would listen as I wrestled with the best way to start the year for my 10th-grade World History students. In their first journal entries, many of my students had already told me they thought history was "boring." I wanted them to see history as something alive that really mattered, filled with the stories of interesting, everyday people. How could I generate some enthusiasm for the past?

At the same time, I was worried about how to integrate curriculum about the war in Iraq. During the lead-up to the U.S. invasion, the topic came up naturally in class. But now students seldom raised it and were often resistant when I brought it up. "We're burned out on Iraq," they told me. How could I teach world history and not explore the current events that were sure to have an enormous impact, both on my students' lives and on the world's future? I knew I didn't want to relegate today's news to a few weeks in June, but I hadn't had much success with such formulaic approaches as current events days or weekly news assignments.

At just that point of confused frustration, I stumbled across an extraordinary resource: *Baghdad Burning, Girl Blog from Iraq* and *Baghdad Burning II*. The author, whose pseudonym is Riverbend, was a young computer programmer in Iraq when the war started. First trapped in her house by the bombings and fighting, then barred from working because of the deteriorating situation of women, she turned to blogging about her everyday life, events in Iraq, and the international situation. These first-person accounts are extraordinarily well-written and compelling (*Baghdad Burning* won the 2005 Lettre Ulysses Award for the Art of Literary Reportage). As an example, here's an excerpt from one of her first blogs, Aug. 21, 2003:

> **"ALGEBRA GOT DISCOVERED IN IRAQ, SO THIS ISN'T JUST IRAQI HISTORY THAT GOT TRASHED, IT'S REALLY WORLD HISTORY."**

MY NEW TALENT

Suffering from a bout of insomnia last night, I found myself in front of the television, channel-surfing. I was looking for the usual—an interesting interview with one of the council, some fresh news, a miracle. . . . Promptly at 2 a.m., the electricity went off and I was plunged into the pitch black hell better-known as "an August night with no electricity in Iraq." So I sat there, in the dark, trying to remember where I had left the candle and matches. After 5 minutes of chagrined meditation, I decided I would 'feel' my way up the stairs and out onto the roof. Step by hesitant step, I stumbled out into the corridor and up the stairs, stubbing a toe on the last step (which wasn't supposed to be there).

(For those of you who don't know, people sleep up on the roof in some of the safer areas because when the electricity goes off, the houses get so hot, it feels like you are cooking gently inside of an oven. The roof isn't much better, but at least there's a semblance of wind.)

A few moments later, my younger brother (we'll call him E.) joined me—disheveled, disgruntled, and half-asleep. We stood leaning on the low wall enclosing the roof watching the street below. I could see the tip of Abu Maan's cigarette glowing in the yard next door. I pointed to it with the words, "Abu Maan can't sleep either." E. grunted with the words, "It's probably Maan." I stood staring at him like he was half-wild—or maybe talking in his sleep. Maan is only 13—how is he smoking? How can he be smoking?

"He's only 13," I stated.

"Is anyone only 13 anymore?" he asked.

I mulled the reality of this remark over. No, no one is 13 anymore. No one is 24 anymore. Everyone is 85 and I think I might be 105. I was too tired to speak and, in spite of his open eyes, I suspected E. was asleep. The silence was shattered a few moments later by the sound of bullets in the distance. It was just loud enough to get your attention, but too far away to be the source of any real anxiety. I tried to determine where they were coming from.

E: How far do you think that is?

Me: I don't know... 'bout a kilometer?

E: Yeah, about.

Me: Not American bullets—

E: No, it's probably from a...

Me: Kalashnikov.

E (impressed): You're getting good at this.

No—I'm getting great at it. I can tell you if it's 'them' or 'us'. I can tell you how far away it is. I can tell you if it's a pistol or machine-gun, tank or armored vehicle, Apache or Chinook. I can determine the distance and maybe even the target. That's my new talent. It's something I've gotten so good at, I frighten myself.

I keep wondering... will an airplane ever sound the same again?

Riverbend's blogs fueled my determination to bring the U.S. war in Iraq into the classroom from the very start. We already had a pre-1500 project planned: a research-based poster on an empire or culture from 1000 to 1500 CE. The project serves as a review of the medieval world and an introduction to research skills, but its most important role is to explore the wealth of extraordinary and diverse cultures in the world before European colonial conquest began in the 1500s. I want to be sure that my students realize that the current division of the world into rich and poor countries, "developed" and "underdeveloped," is a result of colonialism.

I decided to use the Abbasid Caliphate in Iraq as an example before the students began their own projects. The Abbasids, who came to power in Iraq in the mid-8th century, established Baghdad as an extraordinary center of intellectual and cultural development. During this "Golden Age" of medieval Iraq, 100,000 architects, craftspeople, and workers built a four-gated "round city" that soon had a population of half a million; Baghdad's House of Wisdom was a center for Muslim and non-Muslim scholars, who collected and translated the known world's knowledge; Muhammad ibn Musa al-Khwarizmi invented algebra; Ibn al-Haytham became the "father of optics" and a pioneer of the modern scientific method; Ibn Sina summarized the medical knowledge of the time; Islamic astronomers perfected the astrolabe and brought it to Europe; Rumi wrote poetry still beloved today.

We spent several days exploring the political, scientific, and literary achievements of the Abbasid Empire, practicing the note-taking skills I wanted them to apply to the pre-1500 project. I created placards with illustrations and a couple of paragraphs of text on each of the topics listed above, and posted them around the room. I told the students they would be working in pairs to create posters representing the achievements of the Abbasid Empire. Then I gave them graphic organizers and asked them to take bullet-point notes on each of the placards. (This activity is adapted from Teachers' Curriculum Institute materials on the medieval world.) Once the posters were finished and presented, we turned our attention to present-day Iraq.

I used "Assignment: Present-Day Baghdad" to make connections between the past and the present, to generate a base level of understanding of the impact of the war on Iraq, to spur critical thinking, and to introduce Riverbend's blog.

I gave the students several class periods to do the readings and answer the questions in their journals. They discussed their responses in small groups and then we talked as a class. The articles about the destruction of the museums had brought me to tears, but I was surprised at how upset the students were. "Algebra got discovered in Iraq," Melanie said, "so this isn't just Iraqi history that got trashed, it's really world history." They were disturbed by the contradictions between Bush's version of reality in Iraq and that portrayed by MECA, particularly the situation for children.

The discussion also revealed the depths of their feelings of powerlessness. "I went on a bunch of antiwar marches," Alan explained. "My sister got arrested when everyone was sitting down in the streets in downtown San Francisco the day after the war started. But none of it made any difference, so now I don't bother. What's the point?" Other students described relatives who had joined the military because it was the only job they could find or the only way they could afford to go to college. It was clear they could easily envision themselves in the same bind.

I described my own participation in the Vietnam antiwar movement, and how many years we fought against the war, to say nothing of how many years the Vietnamese fought for their own independence. But I could see that I had my work cut out for me: throughout the year, I needed to keep coming back to resistance, especially successful resistance. As progressive teachers, it's so easy to build a case against injustice; it's much harder to develop enthusiasm and confidence about fighting for justice.

The first step was to build my students' connections to Riverbend. I gave students more excerpts from *Baghdad Burning I* and *II* and showed them how to find her blog on the internet. Then I demonstrated how to set up a dialogue journal and gave them the "Dialogue Journal for Baghdad Burning" assignment sheet.

A week later, we met to discuss the dialogue journals. I divided the class into groups of four. I asked each group to choose a facilitator and also a scribe to write the quotes on newsprint. Then each member of the group took a turn or two suggesting a quote for the group to discuss. After the groups had discussed at least four quotes, they picked a quote to share with the class.

Baghdad Burning provided a context to discuss many of the complex issues raised by the war, including the impact on women and children. The girls, in particular, were outraged by the changes in Riverbend's life: she could no longer work or even go outside by herself. We understood all too vividly the daily struggle to deal with the broken water system, lack of electricity, omnipresent death, and constant fear of physical attacks at home and on the street. Riverbend's description of the impact of the war in polarizing Iraqi society was a sharp challenge to all of our media-influenced images of Sunni and Shi'a sectors long at each other's throats.

Throughout the discussions, it was clear that the students could imagine Riverbend as a big sister or a friend. No longer was the war in Iraq a distant abstraction. I felt I had succeeded in making the connection between "historical events" and the lives of individual people and families. As we threw ourselves into an intense year of exploring the Renaissance; Colonial Conquest; French, Russian and Chinese Revolutions; and two World Wars—all the complex eras that comprised World History—I made a promise to myself to continue searching out first-person sources, to continue tying current day issues to the history we were studying, and to stress the role of everyday people in creating history. ▪

Jody Sokolower (jody@rethinkingschools.org) is the managing editor for Rethinking Schools. This article originally appeared in the Winter 2009-10 issue of Rethinking Schools.

Resources

Riverbend's blogs are anthologized in:

Riverbend. *Baghdad Burning: Girl Blog from Iraq.* New York: The Feminist Press at the City University of New York, 2005. Excerpts reprinted with permission.

Riverbend. *Baghdad Burning II: More Girl Blog from Iraq.* New York: The Feminist Press at the City University of New York, 2006.

The entire blog is archived online at: http://riverbendblog.blogspot.com

Wiltenburg, Mary and Philip Smucker. "Looters Plunder in Minutes Iraq's Millennia-Old Legacy," *Christian Science Monitor* 14 April 2003. (www.csmonitor.com/2003/0414/p08s02-wome.html)

Aldiner, Charles. "Rumsfeld Denies U.S. Blame for Iraq Museum Blunder." Reuters 15 April 2003. (http://www.museum-security.org/03/051.html)

Middle East Children's Alliance: www.mecaforpeace.org

Teachers' Curriculum Institute. *History Alive: The Medieval World and Beyond.* New York: TCI, 2005.

Riverbend Blog Excerpt

Over 65 percent of the Iraqi population is unemployed.

… The story of how I lost my job isn't unique. It has actually become very common—despondently, depressingly, unbearably common. It goes like this:

I'm a computer science graduate. Before the war, I was working in an Iraqi database/software company located in Baghdad as a programmer/network administrator (yes, yes … a geek).

No matter what anyone heard, females in Iraq were a lot better off than females in other parts of the Arab world (and some parts of the Western world—we had equal salaries!). We made up over 50 percent of the working force. We were doctors, lawyers, nurses, teachers, professors, deans, architects, programmers, and more. We came and went as we pleased. We wore what we wanted (within the boundaries of the social restrictions of a conservative society).

… During the first week of June, I heard my company was back in business [after the bombing and invasion of Iraq]. It took several hours, seemingly thousands of family meetings, but I finally convinced everyone that it was necessary for my sanity to go back to work.

… The moment I walked through the door, I noticed it. Everything looked shabbier somehow—sadder. The maroon carpet lining the hallways was dingy, scuffed, and spoke of the burden of a thousand rushing feet. The windows we had so diligently taped prior to the war were cracked in some places and broken in others … dirty all over. The lights were shattered, desks overturned, doors kicked in, and clocks torn from the walls.

… My little room wasn't much better off than the rest of the building. The desks were gone, papers all over the place. But A. was there! I couldn't believe it—a familiar, welcoming face. He looked at me for a moment, without really seeing me, then his eyes opened wide and disbelief took over the initial vague expression. He congratulated me on being alive, asked about my family and told me that he wasn't coming back after today. Things had changed. I should go home and stay safe. He was quitting—going to find work abroad.

… A. and I left the room and started making our way downstairs. We paused on the second floor and stopped to talk to one of the former department directors. I asked him when he thought things would be functioning; he wouldn't look at me. His eyes stayed glued to A.'s face as he told him that females weren't welcome right now—especially females who "couldn't be protected." He finally turned to me and told me, in so many words, to go home because 'they' refused to be responsible for what might happen to me.

… I cried bitterly all the way home—cried for my job, cried for my future, and cried for the torn streets, damaged buildings, and crumbling people.

—Riverbend, Sunday, Aug. 24, 2003

Dialogue Journal for *Baghdad Burning*

ASSIGNMENT

As you read Baghdad Burning, keep track of passages you want the class to come back to for discussion. Write your reaction to these passages. Here is how to create a dialogue journal:

- Set up a few pages in your journal labeled Baghdad Burning. Don't forget to note the date and title of the entry you are reading.

- Draw a line down the center of each page. Label the left column Observations/Quotes. Label the right column Reactions and Reflections.

- As you find thought-provoking passages in the text, quote or summarize them in the left column. Then respond or react on the right.

- You should have at least 10 entries. Reactions and Reflections should be at least a paragraph each. I want to see what you are thinking and feeling—don't rush!

Here are some of the things I would like you to look for. This is by no means an exclusive list. The whole point is to generate discussion—so take note of the things that you'd like to talk about.

1. **Everyday Life in Baghdad**—How has the war affected Riverbend's family and neighbors? What do you think Baghdad was like before the war? How has it changed?

2. **Women and the War**—What does Riverbend say about the impact of the war on women in particular? What are your thoughts about that?

3. **Questions**—Take note when you don't understand something in a passage or have questions about its significance. Does Riverbend refer to people or events that we need to know more about?

4. **Future of Iraq**—What does Riverbend think and feel about the future of her country? How are her goals different from those of the U.S. government? The Iraqi leadership?

5. **Resistance**—How do Riverbend and other people in Baghdad try to fight for what they think is right? What are your thoughts and feelings about their choices?

6. **Great Writing**—This is history class, but it's always good to recognize great writing. Usually we associate great writing with fiction or poetry, but nonfiction writing counts, too. What examples can you find of excellent writing in Riverbend's work?

Present-Day Baghdad

ASSIGNMENT

We looked at historical records, original sources, and artwork from Baghdad during the Abbasid Dynasty. We will return to Iraq at different points this year, but I want us to take a little time to talk about Baghdad since the current war began in 2003.

There are four sets of readings:

- Two articles on the destruction of Baghdad's museums during the US invasion
- MECA (Middle East Children's Alliance) description of Baghdad since the war began
- Recent speech by [then-President Bush] on "progress in Iraq"
- Excerpts from Baghdad Burning (blog by Riverbend, a young woman living in Baghdad during the war)

For each set of readings, answer the following questions (please think about these questions and answer in depth):

1. Who is talking?

2. Where did they get their information? Does it seem biased (one-sided) to you? Explain how or why.

3. How do they describe the situation? (This can be in bullet points, but should include at least 5 important details.)

4. How do you think this person (or organization) feels about the importance of Baghdad's history as a cultural center?

5. What do you think this person (or organization) hopes for the future of Baghdad? What would they see as a positive outcome of the war?

Answer these questions at the end:

6. What are your thoughts and feelings about the readings? Which reading or readings struck you as particularly important? Why?

7. What do you see as the best way forward? What should we do to resolve the situation in Baghdad (and Iraq in general)?

Afghanistan's Ghosts

Activities provide background for teaching *The Kite Runner*

IAN MCFEAT

Khaled Hosseini's novel *The Kite Runner* is almost certainly the most popular book about Afghanistan ever published in the United States. And increasingly it's being adopted in high schools across the country. But *The Kite Runner* is not simply a bestselling novel "set" in Afghanistan. It's about a region of the world at war. As an English teacher, I knew that I couldn't teach *The Kite Runner* without first grounding students in a history of the social conflicts there that framed the novel.

The Kite Runner is a powerful personal narrative of a young boy growing up in Kabul, Afghanistan, and the lengths he takes to escape his guilt. The story hinges around a horrific episode in which the main character, Amir, watches silently as his best friend, Hassan, is raped. This wrenching incident haunts Amir throughout his life and touches on themes of privilege, power, inequality, guilt, forgiveness, redemption, and hope that I thought my students would find compelling. But I was concerned about the novel's limited depiction of the social conflicts and wars that had gripped much of the country for decades—and about the Hollywood-type clichés that thread through the novel. For example, *The Kite Runner* offers a contrived and cartoonish plot twist with the former boy rapist, Assef, growing up to be a Big Bad Taliban thug—suggesting implicitly that the Taliban are simply evil, requiring no analysis about their social origins.

> ONE OF MY GOALS IN THE UNIT WAS TO MAKE THE LIVES OF THE PEOPLE OF AFGHANISTAN REAL FOR MY STUDENTS SO THAT THEY MIGHT FEEL COMPASSION AND UNDERSTAND THE HUMAN COST OF WAR.

Such caricatures may offer comforting justification for today's U.S. military involvement there, but they do a disservice to our students. I want my language arts curriculum to move us closer to the real world. I hope my students will recognize the importance of searching for the roots of social problems, and come to feel themselves connected to the lives of others across time and political boundaries, not beholden to Hollywood plot lines.

Of course, the history of Afghanistan is complex, and much more could and should be taught than I'm able to do in my 11th-grade Language Arts classes. Here, I describe two of the activities I used to provide my students some of the background knowledge I thought they would need while reading *The Kite Runner*. I first describe an adaptation of Sandra Childs' activity where students write from photographs taken after the post-September 11, 2001, U.S. bombing campaign in Afghanistan. I also describe a tea party activity I taught prior to beginning the novel that introduced themes and characters from The Kite Runner—as well as themes and characters missing from the novel.

THE FIRST DAY

On the first day of the unit I asked students to reflect in writing about this question I'd written on the board: "When you hear the country name, Afghanistan, what comes to mind?"

I gave students markers and asked them to write their responses on poster paper. Most were vague: "Afghanistan is far away," "The women there are treated bad with masks," "I think it's near Africa or something," and my favorite, "Afghanistan? Like with the war and stuff there?" I used this activity not to amuse myself—I also didn't know much about Afghanistan before I decided to study it with my class—but to find out what students already knew. I anticipated that at least one student would mention the current war in Afghanistan, and so I decided on an activity to follow this pre-assessment.

In a *Rethinking Schools* interview with Portland teacher Sandra Childs (Vol. 17, No. 4) she suggested an idea to allow students, as she said, to "[get] inside the imagined lives of these people and…honor, acknowledge, and voice their suffering." This was one of my goals in the unit: to make the lives of the people of Afghanistan real for my students so that they might feel compassion and understand the human cost of war. Taking Childs' advice and her website suggestion, http://www.dqc.org/~ben/index3.htm, I reserved computer time for my English class in the library. Before I gave each student the URL, I told them that they would be seeing some photographs that were disturbing and showed some of the horrors of war. I let them know that the images were taken in the aftermath of the U.S. bombing campaign in Afghanistan following September 11, 2001. I asked students to choose one photo that touched them or that they found particularly powerful.

I waited and watched students' reactions as they pulled up the war images onto their computers. Some, like Donete, turned away from the screen when the website came up. "I don't want to see that, man," he said. "McFeat, I know what you want me to get here. War is horrible." Kourtney was shocked. "We did this?" she asked her classmate, Heidi, sitting next to her.

Students used most of our class time viewing the 63 pictures from the website. When students had selected their photographs, I told them that they were going to write interior monologues, the inner thoughts and feelings of the individuals in their picture—trying to imagine that they were the people in the photographs.

Students worked on drafts of their interior monologues the next day in class, and we spent time revising and editing the following day. Once students had typed out their final copies, we gathered for a read-around. Kourtney wanted to read her piece first. She'd written hers as a poem:

The Earth Splits Open

Lying here quiet, tender in my arms
I touch your sweet face
So innocent
in slumber
a tear splashes as I cry in disbelief.
Loneliness envelops me
Darkness to the dusk.
Anguish wild, like horses on the run.

Why did this happen to you?
Why couldn't it be me bitten
by the snake of retaliation?
Why don't you get a chance to live?

I am lost and confused,
a whirlwind of fear.
Do I really have to do this?

The earth splits open beneath me,
I have slipped through the crack.
How can a father ever bury his son?

Jessie read his piece with anger:

"Keep the faith, the redemption at the end is worth the suffering." I laughed. Is any god worth all this suffering? Everywhere you look, buildings are blown to dust like a child kicking over a sandcastle. Countless bodies lie in the streets. The air is filled with cries of agony from people who lost loved ones. Those who were unfortunate enough to survive pray for strength to carry on and look towards the sky for answers. But I already know the answer to this so-called "justice." I look to myself and nothing else for the strength to carry on.

Jessie wasn't the only one in class angry about the chaos caused by the bombing campaigns. Others expressed similar sentiments. But I also wanted to hook students into the history of Afghanistan, to have them try on the personalities that began these conflicts years ago. While the pictures offered powerful glimpses into the lives of Afghans devastated by U.S. bombing, the teaching was limited. To truly understand the online photographs, students needed to explore the historical context that led to these situations. With this in mind, I wanted to alert students to characters in *The Kite Runner* before we read about them. Together with a senior civics teacher, Travis Davio, we planned an activity to bring the history of Afghanistan alive for our students. We created a tea party.

THE TEA PARTY'S POLITICAL GHOSTS

Sometimes referred to as a scavenger hunt, (see Linda Christensen's *Reading, Writing, and Rising Up*) a "tea party" can be effective in bringing hidden histories to life. In the tea party, students receive character descriptions and then must attempt to become the characters and introduce themselves to other classmates as a means of building background knowledge before reading a novel, watching a film, or encountering a new unit or any body of difficult material. Travis and I had created roles for each character in the novel, both young and old, as well as characters not included in the text.

For example, *The Kite Runner* does not describe U.S. government interests in the region or corporate interests in the oil and gas reserves of the countries bordering Afghanistan. I wanted students to grapple with the destructive policies of both the U.S. and the Soviet Union and surrounding neighbors of Afghanistan that contributed to the country's painful decline. Over 29 years of war created five and a half million refugees, half a million injured, and left a million for dead. About half of Afghanistan's prewar population of 12 to 15 million were maimed, made homeless, or killed; more than half the villages were destroyed.

So how did this all take place?

In 1979, the Soviets invaded Afghanistan. And, in the 1980s, after the invasion, the U.S. systematically set out to destroy the Soviet-backed state of Afghanistan. I wanted to alert students to the crucial role the U.S. played in bringing terrorists and fundamentalists to power in Afghanistan—a process that began even before the Soviet invasion. These policies still reverberate today.

In the late 1970s, U.S. policy in the region was to bleed the Soviets through a proxy war—which dragged on until the Soviets withdrew in 1989. After the collapse of the Soviet Union, U.S. attention shifted away from the region. Back in Afghanistan, fundamentalists filled the void left in the wake of the cold war. With thick stockpiles of weapons and funding from both the U.S. and the Soviets, Afghan radicals fought over the political scraps left after the Soviet withdrawal. With brutal and devastating results, much of Afghanistan was reduced to rubble. During this devastation in the 1990s, the Western media and governments mostly ignored Afghan civilians.

To alert students to some of this history, Travis and I created what we called "ghost characters." The idea was that the ghost characters would provide students information that the novel leaves out. For instance, the novel doesn't explore the now well-documented U.S. funding and support for development of radical Islamic fundamentalist groups like the Taliban. Similarly, the novel offers historical background on the Soviet invasion of Afghanistan, but fails to discuss the U.S. maneuvering that induced the Soviets to invade. (Jimmy Carter's National Security Advisor, Zbigniew Brzezinski, later bragged in an interview that, contrary to popular myth, the United States started providing weapons to the Mujahadeen in Afghanistan even before the Soviet invasion—a boast confirmed in former CIA director, now Secretary of Defense, Robert Gates' memoir.) I hoped to have students begin to formulate historical questions that might cut into the dominant narrative of Afghanistan: that the bad Russians invaded and the good U.S. stopped them by supporting Afghan "freedom fighters" (and boycotting the 1980 Moscow Olympics). I hoped that the questions students raised about this history might spark them to read the novel more critically and create an openness to investigate this silenced history in more detail later in our unit.

THE TEA PARTY

Instead of announcing the ghost characters' presence at the tea party, Travis and I gave these roles to students on the sly, and had them help serve the tea, while working in character.

One of these behind-the-scenes characters was the Unocal Oil Executive:

John J. Maresca,
Vice President of International
Relations, Unocal

While you or your company aren't mentioned in the novel, you are important to the story of Afghanistan. As an executive at Unocal (a powerful energy company), you work closely with U.S. officials. You testified before Congress in 1998 that the United States needed to change the government in Afghanistan so that a new leader might help you to put through an oil pipeline deal. The novel doesn't mention you, but you exist behind the scenes, pulling strings so that your oil and energy concerns are heard.

We also introduced other characters responsible for plunging Afghanistan into war:

Hamid Karzai,
Unocal, President of Afghanistan

Your name is Hamid Karzai. You used to work for Unocal, the oil company that tried to search for a natural gas pipeline deal in Afghanistan. In 2002, you became President of Afghanistan with help from the Bush Administration. Under your watch, a new pipeline deal with Unocal was signed that brought positive change to your country. You see yourself as a renaissance man, someone with ties to Washington, D.C., and the U.S. government, that will ultimately help your country. While you were never mentioned in The Kite Runner, you still had an enormous impact on the history of Afghanistan.

We listed the known characters from the novel on the white board, but on students' tea party handouts, we included a few questions to alert them to the "Ghosts" in the room:

Which characters in the room are NOT included in the novel? If you haven't found one, ask around and try to discover who they are. What role does each of these characters play in Afghan history? Why do you think they weren't included in this novel?

Jessica had her "Amir" card in hand when she met Hamid Karzai, played by Donete. "So, what do you have to do with this novel?" she asked.

Donete said flatly, "Nothing. They don't have me in this book. But I am President of Afghanistan, and I used to work for Unocal."

Jessica walked over to where I was serving tea. "I got one of the ghosts, McFeat," she said while writing Karzai's information down in her packet.

Peter found a ghost character of his own. "That Brazaki [Brzezinski] guy helped to start the whole wars and stuff between the U.S.S.R. and us. Go talk to Samantha, she'll tell you."

After students had their fill of tea and cookies, and after they'd mingled around, and introduced themselves to other characters, I had them return to their seats and fill out responses to questions that I had prepared and copied off into packets. I also gave them time to write down questions they now had about Afghan history after having done the tea party. I wanted students to revisit their assumptions about Afghanistan and begin overturning some of the stereotypes they may have carried into the unit. And I also wanted students to begin formulating ideas and questions of their own that would help our critical thinking about the sometimes hidden history of Afghanistan.

Of course, I didn't expect students to digest all of this history during the tea party, but I hoped that student questions raised during this activity would help launch an inquiry in conjunction with reading The Kite Runner—an inquiry that would be grounded in students' curiosity.

QUESTIONS

Student questions revealed some of this thinking. After we had shared their questions aloud, following the tea party, I read them over that night:

▪ So why does this Brzezinski guy want the Soviets in Afghanistan so bad?
▪ Is this Unocal deal why we have to pay so much for oil? It costs me like, 20 dollars for a half tank of gas. So how does this work?
▪ What exactly was the war between the U.S. and Soviets?
▪ Why were we in Afghanistan in the 70s and then later?
▪ Why didn't the U.S. just quit sending money?

These and other questions provided a baseline for students to begin our investigation of Afghan history while reading The Kite Runner. Yet the questions also revealed some holes in the tea party. Most revealed my students' desire to search for the easier responses that seek individual culprits for these wars, rather than to search out broader social interests. As tea parties focus on individual historical narratives, this kind of activity inherently lends itself to narrower explanations for U.S. policy. Reviewing kids' responses made me see that I needed to add pieces to this curriculum that would help students recognize the broader social and systemic factors that drive policy decisions that lie behind the conflicts in Afghanistan. For example, I needed to have activities that addressed the Cold War between the Soviet Union and the U.S. in Afghanistan. And I needed activities that explored the gap between rhetoric and reality of the post-9/11 bombing of Afghanistan.

And yet, the tea party worked well in other ways. The questions helped students recognize that there was more to Afghan history than they would encounter in The Kite Runner—lots more. Ultimately, pursuing the questions that students raised following the tea party allowed us to dig deeper into the themes The Kite Runner addresses, but also to reach beyond the novel.

For instance, the student questions about the role of the Soviet Union and the U.S. in the Cold War was clearly a historical area with which students had not yet grappled. And this made it clear that we needed to teach about this conflict as we were reading The Kite Runner.

WHAT WAS GOING ON HERE?

A powerful aspect of *The Kite Runner* is that it presents a human face for a region of the world that has far too often been labeled and misunderstood. *The Kite Runner* helps us to see Afghans as real people, with lives, interests, shame, guilt—human conditions that connect us all. With the tea party as background, when we got into the novel we were able to chart characters by political representations, analyzing the book not just in traditional literary terms, but also in broader political and historical terms. And we compared themes from the book with themes from our own society. For example, we looked closely at the relationship of Amir and his father, Baba, and compared and contrasted this relationship with the one President Bush has with the U.S. population. We pulled out quotes from Baba and compared and contrasted these with quotes from Bush's speeches about Afghanistan. We also pulled out quotes from the book that touched on the history of Afghanistan and had students research and rewrite those sections with a more adequate depiction of the history that Afghan civilians struggled through.

As I indicated earlier, *The Kite Runner* falls into the dominant narrative about the region: good guy versus bad guy, us against them. And coupled with the media's failure to question U.S. military involvement in Afghanistan, the idea that evil must be expunged from the earth, the notion that conflict can be solved with gun power and burning shards from missiles and bombs, *The Kite Runner* can become a problematic book to teach.

Yet, despite its shortcomings, *The Kite Runner* can also open up avenues for valuable social and personal exploration with students. With a curriculum crafted with the politics of the region in mind, dedicated to investigating the motives behind the wars in Afghanistan, our students can move closer to thinking critically about U.S. foreign policy and the role that novels play in the consciousness of our nation. ∎

Ian McFeat (imcfeat@msn.com) teaches Social Studies and Language Arts at Lincoln High School's ABE academy in Tacoma, Wash. This article originally appeared in the Fall 2008 issue of Rethinking Schools.

Portland to Palestine

A student-to-student project evokes empathy and curiosity

KEN GADBOW
RETHINKING SCHOOLS (Winter 2009)

When asked to synthesize 16 weeks of study on the Israeli-Palestinian conflict, covering dozens of readings, films, role plays, guest speakers, and discussions, the high school students in my Middle East Studies class at Trillium Charter School in Portland, Ore., quickly organized a nine-point list of the most important topics and activities. All but one were related to the Mercy Corps' Why Not program, an internet-based exchange run by the international humanitarian relief organization (also based in Portland). My students' real-time interactions with their counterparts in the West Bank and Gaza made real the suffering and daily lives of people their own age living in conflict, and challenged them to consider the responsibilities of global citizenry.

Why Not, now part of Mercy Corps' partner organization Global Citizen Corps, began as an informal email exchange program between students in northern Iraq and Taiwan in 2003, facilitated by Mercy Corps, and has grown to encompass over 600 youth in the United States, United Kingdom, Lebanon, Jordan, Iraq, and the Palestinian Territories, corresponding through two-way blog and live video conferences. The "Why Not" label was coined by a group of students organizing a Mercy Corps-supported community newsletter in Beirut in 2005. Plagued by pessimism about the potential impact of their efforts, some were suggesting that they should abandon the project altogether, when one eager, hopeful participant blurted out, "Lesh la?"—Arabic for "Why not?" The words became the name of the group's newsletter and later of the Mercy Corps program itself.

Why Not was dropped in my lap in the spring of 2007, just a few weeks before summer break. Mercy Corps was looking for some flexible partners who wanted to work with youth in the Palestinian Territories. I had done no previous teaching on the Middle East, and was relatively uninformed about Palestine-Israel. I was aware that the United States was a supporter of Israel, that presidents from Carter to Bush II had been involved in peace efforts, and that the U.S. media frequently portrayed Palestinians as violent aggressors, but I did not know much more. I took the opportunity to learn along with my students.

The Why Not experience involves on-line discussions, loosely moderated by teacher-facilitators, and videoconferences using web-cams, microphones, and LCD projectors. Mercy Corps helps teachers get started, but the process is relatively simple: The blogging portion is simpler than using Facebook, and the video portion can be run from common applications like Skype. During the

I WANTED STUDENTS TO THINK ABOUT THE FRAMEWORKS THAT THE MEDIA FASHIONS FOR US—THE PURELY BAD GUYS AND THE PURELY GOOD GUYS, THE CLEANSING ROLE OF VIOLENCE, THE CONTEMPT FOR NON-WESTERN CULTURES.

videoconferences, participants can generally all see each other on the screen at the same time as students take turns in front of the microphone, posing and responding to questions and ideas.

Six countries have students taking part in internet and video exchanges facilitated by Mercy Corps. The Palestinian Territories are among them; Israel is not. We talk a lot in class about the need to balance perspectives. We frequently turn to news reports from the Jerusalem Post, Haaretz, and the Israeli government to look at events from different positions. My students are captivated by the experience of speaking directly with young people living in war, but it is not simply the Palestinians who become real to them, it is the whole conflict, it is the reality of war itself. People are suffering. People are living in fear. Israeli kids riding buses are living in fear. Palestinians whose homes might be bulldozed are living in fear. Children, Israelis and Palestinians, trying to get to school are living in fear. Students get that.

Why Not is a tool for forging understanding. Since my initial experience with the program, I regularly teach units or whole classes on the Middle East and use Why Not as a centerpiece of these experiences. I have students participate in Why Not blogging and videoconferences, in part, for the "wow" factor, the "Oh my God, I can't believe we are actually speaking to people in Gaza" factor. I do it for my student who produces no work, yet who keeps coming to class because this issue has become real to him. It is not from the news or from the teacher. It is looking you straight in the eye. It is laughing with you, telling you jokes, rapping in Arabic. It is human connection. During the first videoconference we, Americans and Palestinians, could not stop laughing. We giggled at the microphone, at the video camera, at the hiccups in the connection. The sheer present-ness of the experience was intoxicating.

TEACHING THE CONFLICT

Most of my students begin their study of the Middle East with little understanding of the Palestinian-Israeli conflict. Few can find the Palestinian Territories on a map and many assume that the violence has been happening "forever," or at least for hundreds or even "thousands" of years. Students understand people are dying, but most cannot identify the belligerents any more than as "terrorists" and "Jews." Before we begin a unit on Palestine-Israel, students study historic persecution of Jews, modern anti-Semitism, and Zionism. We do an extensive unit on the Holocaust, reading Elie Wiesel's *Night* as well as *Maus* by Art Spiegelman. We discuss and write about what it means to live amidst pervasive fear and uncertainty. We transition into the Palestinian conflict by looking at complementary accounts of the history of the region from the early 1900s. Students analyze perspectives, identify biases, and try to understand motivation from both Palestinian and Israeli perspectives. We later use a role play developed by Jeff Edmundson about the United Nations 1947 decision that established the state of Israel to help students identify some of the players in the conflict. Students tackle the perspectives of Zionist Jews, Palestinian Muslims, the British government, the U.S. government, and the United Nations. Through their characters' perspectives, students craft plausible arguments that describe the needs of their group, and propose a solution that will provide safety and security to those involved.

While students are getting to know their Palestinian counterparts through on-line introductions in Why Not, they continue to study the conflict in the classroom. We use a tea party based on characters from Deborah Ellis' book *Three Wishes*, a terrific collection of interviews with Israeli and Palestinian youth, to help students understand the perspectives of children living in the conflict. The culminating project for the class is the negotiation of a peace plan from the perspective of a character from the powerful 2001 film *Promises* by B.Z. Goldberg. Like *Three Wishes*, *Promises* introduces its audience to young Palestinians and Israelis affected by the conflict. Students in my class advocate for their assigned positions through a role play written by Bill Bigelow.

Through the *Promises* role play, students draw connections between the isolation of Gaza and the destruction of Palestinian homes, and U.S. financial contributions to the state of Israel. Trillium students were shocked that the United States grants more than $8 million per day in foreign aid to Israel. Many students advocate in class for a more active U.S. role in ending the violence; some are outraged that the United States is funding the conflict. Many of the students' proposed solutions to the violence include the United States providing financial compensation to Palestinians. Through role play, students demonstrate their understanding of the intensity with which various sides of the conflict approach the issue. Voices rise during debate over settlements in the West Bank, proposed borders and boundaries, and the status of Jerusalem, among other topics. As students pack up their things after day two of the *Promises* role play, I overhear a telling exchange: "Wow. That was exciting." "Yeah, I am just glad nobody got punched."

Learning about Palestine-Israel rattles the ease with which students let headlines pass by. They experience how hard it is to abandon someone once they get to know them. That is the point of *Promises*. That is the point of *Three Wishes*, and that is the point of Why Not. When the suffering is embodied and not theoretical, we are forced to confront it. In this conflict, the suffering is concentrated and the issue is polarized. Students ask family and friends about Palestine-Israel and are surprised to discover how heated it gets. They are able to make tangible connections between what they see on the news, what they hear from their Palestinian counterparts, and what we study in the classroom.

STUDENTS SHARE THEIR LIVES

U.S. students participating in Why Not learn about issues affecting the daily lives of their counterparts through Palestinian blog posts like "The Water Crisis in the Palestinian Territories," "Gaza Siege Causing Major Health Crisis," and "Gaza Facing Humanitarian Crisis." But not all topics are so heavy. In fact, most of them aren't. Students spend weeks on conversations based around the question "What do you do for fun?" They discuss the stuff of youth: music, sports, food, movies, and pastimes. Participants share "I Am From" poems; post photo-essays; ask questions about family life, boyfriends, and girlfriends; and slowly move into more challenging discussions.

One such discussion was provoked by a video created by Palestinian youth, titled *Lostland* and posted under the label "West Bank Meets Gaza," that chronicles a letter writing campaign in which elementary students in the West Bank wrote and drew pictures to express sympathy and solidarity with their counterparts in Gaza. These personal perspectives, combined with their historical knowledge and what they learned about the Israeli assault, helped Trillium students grasp the geographic and political divides separating Israel, the West Bank, and Gaza.

The directness of the exchange seems to have the greatest impact on the students. Many students speak of the program as "breaking barriers" and "opening doors."

Chris, a senior, remarked on the contrast between Why Not and "watching CNN or any news channel we have":

> There is an alternative, and that is what we're engaged in. And that is having Palestinians on this screen talking to you in this room, and you talking right back to them....That is a huge difference from having some third party, some other group of people talk about another group of people. Why not just have them tell you themselves?

Once students have established a rapport online, they express their personal experiences directly to one another, as in "Gaza is Dying," written by Salam, living in Gaza in March 2008:

> We are now in Gaza living in a very bad condition, there is no fuel for cars and my father stopped [driving] due to lack of fuel, we go to school with great difficulty, this is only regarding fuel, in terms of health and medication for patients in the latest attack of the Israeli army injured nearly 350 people sent them to Egypt, this is just another week under the siege. There is no Coca-Cola for example, there is no children's milk, there is no drinking water. [There is] contaminated water. There is no electricity.... I write quickly so as not to break the electricity and what I wrote goes, every day studying in the daytime, because I do not [expect] electricity at night. In spite of poverty, prices are tripled, the salaries are so low and the prices of the goods are higher than Europe.

This particular post garnered a dozen direct responses from my students, including this one from Ian:

> Thank you for this new post. Every piece of information on this website I read leads me a little bit closer to comprehending what is really happening over there. I wish that there was more that I could do to help. It must take a lot of courage and perseverance to get through what you are going through every day. I hope to God that your situation will improve.

After another participant in Gaza posted a particularly detailed account about living with limited electricity and fuel, one of my students posted a response titled "This Must Stop":

> After reading "Darkness in Gaza" I cannot even begin to address my feelings about this crisis. Knowing now that the situation is even worse, this worries me and I think about it a lot. If people don't see people as people, but as things, as a meaningless life, I don't know if I will have any faith in humanity. Here we live in such luxury, such privilege, but that doesn't mean that we are apathetic to your struggles. What is happening, to me sounds like genocide, resources cut off and a deliberate destruction of your country. We feel for you, we want to help. What is happening is inexcusable and inhumane. I wish we

had more power over our government so that we could send aid to you or help find a solution. But for now, we can talk, we can communicate, we can send you our thoughts and you can share your thoughts with us. Let us bridge this gap of ignorance and let the whole world know that these atrocities will not be tolerated.

Let there be peace, understanding and love for all beings.   —Fiona

When directly confronted with the daily suffering of people their own age, students readily access empathy and compassion, which may be combined with a sense of guilt or culpability. Students had a chance to confront this issue while preparing for a videoconference in which one of the topics was educational access. The Trillium students were at first reluctant to be critical of U.S. schools, for fear of appearing ungrateful in front of their counterparts, who are at times kept from attending school altogether due to interference by the occupying Israeli military and the prevalence of Israeli Defense Force checkpoints. As the Trillium students began to address these issues individually, they described an American school system in which wealth, race, ethnicity, and language were clear factors in academic achievement. My students became excited, rather than embarrassed, to convey what they saw as systematic injustice within the United States when talking to the students in Gaza. Palestinian students were surprised to learn that there is such disparity in the United States in access to resources between schools in wealthy areas and schools in poor areas.

LASTING CONNECTIONS

During the spring of 2009, I was working with a Why Not group, some of whom had been part of the program for over a year. We had connected with various groups in the West Bank and Gaza, and had the good fortune to have a few consistent West Bank and Trillium students establish a relationship. Having students recognize each other in a videoconference is inspiring. Noticeable shivers pass among the participants and most of us wind up giggling, even at seven o'clock in the morning.

The Trillium students then had the chance to work with a new group in the West Bank. We had some problems with the connection during our first videoconference, which resulted in poor and occasionally disrupted video feed. Students quickly resorted to instant messaging (a seamless transition for them) and emailing photos in order to continue the dialogue. The

first meeting was largely one of introductions and getting acquainted.

Shortly after that meeting, several of my students decided to take part in a rally in downtown Portland to protest the Israeli invasion of Gaza. They created a giant banner with "Why Not Peace Now?" written in Arabic and English and a Palestinian flag with a peace sign superimposed over it. They marched in the cold rain, chanting, chatting, and feeling empowered. A week or so after the march, Trillium students had their second videoconference with the West Bank group.

The Palestinian students began by presenting us with a gift. They had written all of our names in Arabic on large paper and showed them to us one by one. We were touched by the gesture, and feeling embarrassed that we had not created something as well to reflect our appreciation, when one student said, "Hey, get the banner!" Two students unrolled it in front of the video camera. The silence that followed was unsettling. We were not sure if they were able to see it well or if our Arabic translation (via web translator) was offensive. Chris went to the microphone and asked if they were seeing it all right. In Palestine, Dhalia approached the microphone and explained that her group was stunned. They were silent, she said, because "We didn't think anyone knew we were here." In a trembling voice, she added, "You even know what our flag is like."

The blog postings and video gatherings foster relationships over what had seemed insurmountable geographic and cultural barriers. This direct communication makes real to students, indeed to all of us involved, that people across the globe can approach delicate issues with compassion and understanding. This creates a tangible access point to understanding an intense and oppressive situation. And students make friends in the process. As Solomon put it, "At the end people do not want to sign off because they are getting along so well, even though it is a friend on the other side of the world that you have never met." ▪

Ken Gadbow (gadbow@gmail.com) teaches at Trillium Charter School in Portland, Ore. For more information on Mercy Corps' internet-based exchange program, visit http://globalcitizencorps.org.

Fahrenheit 9/11: Silent Discussion

Students reflect on thought-provoking subject matter prior to class discussion

JULIE O'NEILL, SANDRA CHILDS, AND BILL BIGELOW

Michael Moore's film *Fahrenheit 9/11* elicits strong feelings of all kinds, and it will be a rare class where tension is absent after viewing the film. As teachers, our challenge is to harness this energy and direct students toward a reasonable conversation. One strategy we have used is the silent discussion. Through silent discussion, all class members are encouraged to respond to a series of quotes, questions, or statements related to a piece of writing, class activity, or film. It offers time for students to reflect and form their own opinions, and the writing space to express them openly. In this case, silent discussion facilitates a deeper analysis of the film and its contents, while allowing students time to engage each other in thoughtful dialogue.

For example, in response to a George W. Bush quote—"We wage war to save a civilization"—Bianca wrote: "Wage war and civilization shouldn't go in the same sentence. There is always an alternative to war." Antonia disagreed: "What about the Revolutionary War, the war against Nazi Germany? Some wars had to be fought." Written discussion continued around these responses, raising critical questions: Who should fight in a war? Is there a point where the U.S. doesn't need to intervene? What should have been the U.S. response to the 9/11 attacks? Silent discussion provided our students an opportunity to highlight and reflect on difficult elements of the film, and served as a springboard for larger class discussions.

MATERIALS AND PREPARATION

1. Select 8-10 important questions, passages, direct quotes, or statements related to the film. Use selections from the list below or generate others from student film notes and previous lessons. Passages should be thought-provoking and push students to expand or clarify their thinking. All quotes here are from *Fahrenheit 9/11* unless otherwise noted:

▪ "The military is an excellent option for young people of Flint" or (your community).

▪ "We wage war to save a civilization." –former President George W. Bush

▪ "You can make people do anything when they're afraid."
   –Democratic Representative Jim McDermott, Washington.
Should Americans be afraid? What should they be afraid of?

- "Al-Qaeda didn't make a decision to send my son to Iraq. Ignorance … people think they know, but they don't. I didn't know and now I've lost my son."
  –Lila Lipscomb
- Should we give up liberties to "fight terrorism" and for "security"?
- "A massive military retaliation causing the deaths of thousands … is the worst possible thing we could do. It would only guarantee an endless supply of fresh terrorists for decades to come. We can have security or we can have revenge. We cannot have both."
  –USAF Lt. Col. Robert M. Bowman, ret.,
  in *The Long and Short of Terrorism and Security*
- "I would throw away the old maxim, 'My country right or wrong,' and instead I would say, 'My country when she is right.' Is dissent patriotic?"
  –Mark Twain, speech reported in the *New York Times*, March 17, 1901.
- "I would not let anyone send me back over there to kill other poor people, especially when they pose no threat to me or my country."
  –Abdul Henderson, U.S. Marine Corps
- "The haves and have mores—some people call you the elite, I call you my base."
  –former President George W. Bush
- Continued warfare in Iraq is "good for business, bad for the people."
  –corporate representative, NewFields.com
- "War happens and then the fighting starts. … We're pumped up and motivated to go … 'the roof, the roof, the roof is on fire.'"
  –U.S. soldier in Iraq
- Disney (Miramax's parent company) refused to allow distribution of *Fahrenheit 9/11* under its name because the company claimed it was too politically slanted. Why would a media company want to distance itself from this film?

2. Write each question or statement on a separate sheet of chart paper. The paper should be large enough so there is plenty of room for student comments.

3. Post pieces of chart paper around the classroom in areas that students can easily access. Use the walls or large tables spread throughout the classroom.

SUGGESTED PROCEDURE

Students will need time to read the prompts and time to respond. Plan for at least five minutes per response for the initial responses (20-25 minutes). After the initial responses to the quotes, students will need additional time to read and react to each other's responses; this is how the dialogue is created. Plan for an additional five minutes per response (15-20 minutes) for this second piece of the silent discussion.

1. Establish expectations for the lesson:
- Students will write on 4-5 passages or questions and will respond to 3-4 other student comments in the activity. Emphasize that they should respond not just to the quotes, but to each other as well.
- Emphasize the silent dialogue. Let students know that conversations should occur on paper only. Class discussion will follow the activity.
- Encourage students to be respectful of the process and each other. There will be disagreements—that is one of the elements of this procedure. Silent discussion is a valuable tool for dealing with controversial issues in a way that invites reflection and calms tempers.
- Students should initial or sign each comment. This way, you can draw attention to specific comments, tease out details, and point to contradictions or areas of consensus. Signing these also tends to limit inappropriate comments.

2. As students travel silently around the room, encourage them to fully explore and clarify their thoughts on paper, not to write one sentence statements or "I agree."

3. After there are initial student responses on most of the posters, ask students to read each other's comments and respond on at least 3-4 of the posters, generating the silent discussion. Again, encourage students to fully explain their own thoughts and to push each other to more clarity.

4. When all students are done, ask them to pick one question or quote that really interests them, or a quote they did not respond to, and continue writing. This buys time for the teacher to travel the room reading the comments to get a sense of class opinions, connections, and points of disagreement before the (verbal) discussion begins. Alternatively, complete the silent discussion on one day and start the verbal discussion the following day.

5. Use the posters to help guide classroom discussion. When we did this, many students wrote on whether dissent was patriotic. Before they could get to the question, students felt the need to clarify what it meant to "support the president." In *Fahrenheit 9/11*, Britney Spears says, "We should trust and support our president." Some students wondered if one could support the president and still oppose his policies. Others argued the most patriotic thing a person can do is dissent. What was remarkable in the discussion was that all voices were present. In a regular classroom conversation, many students tend to disappear. In this activity everyone was scrambling to get their word in. As the discussion progresses, students begin to build, pull from and connect ideas. If some students don't participate in the discussion after the "silent discussion," refer to a comment they wrote and invite them in to explain and clarify.

6. Leave the posters up in the room to use as prompts for an essay or metaphorical drawing, and to encourage further silent discussion. ▪

Fahrenheit 9/11: Thinking in Pictures, Feeling in Words

Creative responses explore ideas and emotions from many perspectives

SANDRA CHILDS, BILL BIGELOW, AND JULIE O'NEILL

*F*ahrenheit 9/11, by filmmaker Michael Moore, tackles complicated issues and is filled with complex information and evocative images. This lesson uses creative writing and art as approaches that encourage students to sort through and give expression to their feelings about this challenging content. Allowing students to respond creatively will add dimension to their intellectual responses and will deepen their critical reflection by highlighting the people, stories, and relationships in the film. Working creatively, either in pictures or in words, also gives students a chance to turn troubling images into instructive art.

This lesson offers students a choice between writing and drawing. Alternatively, the teacher may decide to offer only one option or to assign both separately.

For the writing option, students may choose to write poetry or interior monologues. Writing allows students to personalize the film. Much of our students' writing after we showed *Fahrenheit 9/11* came directly from their own lives, including two of our students who wrote about loved ones in the military headed for Iraq.

Creative writing allows students to explore the thoughts and feelings of the people in the film and come to a deeper understanding of others' perspectives. An interior monologue requires the student to exercise imagination, to wonder what is going on inside someone's head during a particular situation: the imagined voice of a child after a bomb destroyed her home or the imagined voice of a conflicted U.S. soldier.

The writing brings those other perspectives to life for classmates who listen to the stories and poems when they are shared at the end of the lesson. A two-dimensional image from the screen turns into a human being with complex emotions. The interior monologue activity can be a good way to "flesh out" the people involved in this conflict and also counter any impulse to dehumanize those with whom we might not agree. Interior monologues do not have to be written just from the voice of human beings. Some of the most startling writing comes from perspectives rarely imagined, like the telephone Lila Lipscomb is holding when she learns her son has been killed, or the Marine recruiting brochure Michael Moore hands to a reluctant Congressman.

Materials Needed:

1. Copies of *"Fahrenheit 9/11:* Writing Models"— one for each student.

2. Copy or overhead transparency of *"Fahrenheit 9/11:* Metaphorical Drawing Model"

3. Copies for students of *"Fahrenheit 9/11:* Suggested Prompts" (optional)

4. Blank paper

5. Crayons, colored pencils, other art materials

Drawing offers students a chance to think in pictures and imagine complex interrelationships. It allows those students who are more visual and less verbal to communicate their understanding in subtle and complicated ways. Students borrow from the film or create their own metaphors to describe the situation. For instance, Kelsey drew a picture of an American inside a box to show how closed off many Americans are from what is really going on in the world. Christina drew a "Paint by Number" mask, borrowing from the make-up sequence at the beginning of the film to critique the media and the government's presentation of war as something pretty.

After completing their creative pieces, students share their work and draw final conclusions based on reading the "collective text" of their classmates. Those conclusions and the pieces themselves can be a springboard for a persuasive essay.

SUGGESTED PROCEDURE

1. Before students watch the film, explain they will have a chance to draw or write when the film is over. As they watch they should note:
   ▪ Key lines they could use in a poem or interior monologue (a writing from the imagined voice/perspective of someone or something in the film).
   ▪ People or things from whose point of view they could write.
   ▪ Images/relationships in the film that they could use as metaphors to describe the situation and the complex connections.

2. Explain the writing option: After the film, pass out a copy of "*Fahrenheit 9/11*: Writing Models" to each student. Use the models to demonstrate good writing. We find that reading the examples is not enough. Ask students to identify in the models some of the elements of good writing, as illustrated below:
   ▪ Explain to the students: "Here are a few examples of poems, interior monologues, and stories written by other high school students who have seen the film. As we read through them, think about other writing possibilities. We will share your ideas out loud with the class."

▪ Read the examples out loud or have students volunteer to read. Ask students to look for "stolen lines"—i.e., words or phrases lifted from *Fahrenheit 9/11*— in the pieces. Ask them to share the ones they find. Tell them that they are encouraged to borrow lines or phrases from the film, too, and use them in their writing.

▪ As they read Andréa Yancey's "Nobody Knows," ask students to look for repeating lines. Encourage the use of repetition in their own poetry to add weight and structure.

▪ After they read Bianca Reynolds' "One Less," explain the two-voice poem (also called a dialogue poem) model. A two-voice poem juxtaposes two complementary or opposing viewpoints or experiences, playing off each other's lines and sometimes sharing the same lines. A two-voice poem highlights the similarities and the differences for two individuals in a particular situation. In this case, Bianca juxtaposed the experiences of the mother of someone in the military and a senator whose child is not in the military. (For another example of a two-voice poem, see "Two Women" in *Rethinking Our Classrooms Vol. I* or "Two Young Women" in *Rethinking Globalization*.)

▪ Ask students to look back through the writings and highlight or underline the concrete imagery (things they can taste, touch, see, feel, hear, smell). Have them share a few examples. Encourage students to use specific images in their writing to make it vivid.

3. Ask students to brainstorm ideas for poems and interior monologues, and make a list on the board or overhead projector. (If your class is unfamiliar with this kind of writing or you think they might have a hard time coming up with ideas, pass out copies of "*Fahrenheit 9/11*: Suggested Prompts" or describe one or two from the list. Most of these were suggested by our students when we brainstormed possibilities after watching the film.)

   If you decide to have students do both of the writing and the drawing options, stop here and have them do their writing. Then, after sharing their writing (steps 7 and 8 below), explain the next part of the activity.

4. Explain and share the metaphorical drawing option:
   ▪ Make sure they understand that a metaphor is a comparison between two dissimilar things (e.g., my life is a river).

▪ Refer to one or two powerful images used in the film—for instance, when Lila Lipscomb talks about her family's history in the military she refers to them as the "backbone of America." Ask students to think about extending that metaphor. If they were to draw that backbone, would it be broken, strong? What would it be attached to? Where would it be? This could turn into a metaphorical drawing.

▪ Share the metaphorical drawing sample with the students. Doug Rickett and Paul Comery's metaphorical drawing "Greed" shows their view of U.S. motives in attacking Iraq. Their explanation reads: "This picture of the world has the fingers of the Americans coming out of the earth. The fingers are clutching, surrounding Iraq as well as the Middle East. Oil is dripping out

Sample metaphorical drawing by Doug Rickett and Paul Comery.

from the cracks surrounding the fingers."

▪ Describe one of the other drawings our students came up with during this activity: Lindsey Ivie called hers "The Spoils of War" and illustrated how the war on terror has resulted in the use of taxpayer dollars to pay for expensive defense contracts that make the rich and well-connected richer. In her drawing,

money travels directly from a blue shirt labeled "Blue-Collar Working Class" into an IV bag filled with blood (also blue) labeled "Blue-Blood Class Elite."

▪ Explain that students should thoroughly label everything so the viewer can "get it" and they should write an explanation on the back. For instance, Lindsey's explanation reads: "Step One: remove money from pocket of average Joe. Step Two: funnel into pockets of nation's elite. Steps may be repeated as needed. May be more effective during simultaneous applications of terror."

5. Ask students to brainstorm ideas for metaphorical drawings and record these on the board.

6. Tell students to allow each other creative space by being quiet. Provide drawing paper and art supplies. Give them at least a half hour. Many students may want to take their work home to finish.

7. Once students have completed their pieces in class or at home, arrange the chairs in a circle and ask students to show and explain their work. Ask students to take notes on important points, repeating images, or insights as their classmates share. You might ask them to record favorite lines or take notes on (and then write about) specific questions:

▪ How does war affect people?

▪ What were the key relationships illustrated in the metaphors?

▪ Where in the pieces did you see or hear hope?

▪ Where in the pieces did you see or hear resistance?

8. Discuss the common images, ideas, and themes and/ or the questions above.

EXTENDING THE LESSON

The interior monologues, poetry, and visual metaphors can also be used to help students write persuasive essays on some aspect of the film or unit. In fact, students sometimes find that without much effort they can turn their metaphorical drawings into thesis statements for their essays. The creative writing can be used as a dramatic introduction to a persuasive essay about war, corporations, the media, military recruiting, or other issues raised in a study of war and terrorism. ▪

Fahrenheit 9/11:
Thinking in Pictures, Feeling in Words

Writing Models

THE EMPTY SOLDIER

When you kill someone you kill part of yourself. I know each day I feel the numbness spread, as I spray green specters with machine gun fire. That's what I do. When the dust clears I watch the space between the crosshairs as stillness slowly descends. I can see sparks of life go up and out of this dead land and a scrap of myself flittering away like ash on the breeze or a moth spiraling into the sky.

What are we doing? I was never meant to see so much blood, so many husks where houses used to be. I'm tired of screaming, tired of shooting, tired of the heat of burning buildings radiating against my skin, tired of the smoke that burns my eyes. I'm tired of my friends who think we are living in a video game and distract themselves with songs and jokes and incessant playing of that roof song. They told me we were coming here to rebuild not to set things on fire and let the "mother-f____r burn." But now that phrase is on repeat in my brain, filling the newly vacated space left behind when my compassion and my understanding and reason left town.

—Andrea Townsend
Earlham College
Richmond, Indiana

NOBODY KNOWS

Nobody knows
until it's too late
& the Marine is on your doorstep
with a folded flag
(those flags are extra starched)

Nobody knows
when your heart stops
& the world stops
& you freeze in place

Nobody knows
how tears somehow become the
blood
of your brother
or your dad
or your mom
or your anybody
and you can taste them
& have them fade
but they never exactly wash away

Nobody knows
except me
& that Marine
in his dress blues
& white gloves
(to say his hands are innocent
of blood)
is standing in front of me
with an extra-starched flag
with a generic apology
arms out
but not holding up
my fallen body
or my fallen brother.

—Andréa Yancey
Franklin High School
Portland, Oregon

GEORGIE PORGIE

Georgie Porgie
puddin' and pie
lied to America
and made people cry
The crying people
were ignored
like the crying soldiers
who killed the crying civilians
death of the mind
in a soldier's head
when he raids the house
following orders

I have a friend
destined for Iraq
Will he become
the soldier for American money?
Risking his life?
Will he kill?
Will he kill?
Will a shrieking woman's crying
be silenced
by a bullet
from a gun
held by him?

Will he stare her in the face
and empty out his soul
revert back to his training
and shut her up?
Will he feel good about it?
Will he look at the crying boy
next to his momma
and see his yet born son?
Will he feel sick?
Will he try to rid his body of evil
by vomiting?
Will the blood and vomit stick to him
like a memory
lingering in the back of his head?
Will he pray
Will he pray
for forgiveness?
Will it be granted?
Or will he drink til his body is numb?
Will he be able to
conceive this horrible thing?

That woman will never
see her son grown
That boy will cry
until he starves to death
He will cry like the mother did
like the soldier who shot her
like the people who were lied to
So I ask you, Georgie Porgie
Do you enjoy it?

—David Gerber
Franklin High School,
Portland, Oregon

ONE LESS

This is a two-voice poem. The bold type is the mother of an enlisted young man and the plain type is a U.S. senator who voted for this war but whose children will not be fighting in it.

I have two children.
I have two children.

One is dead.
Both are alive.

He fought for freedom.
They live in freedom.

I told him to enlist.
I made sure my kids did not enlist.

I couldn't afford their college.
I paid for them to stay home.

A war of lies.
A war of lies.

All for oil.
All for money.

I lost everything.
I lost nothing.

Freedom is gone.
More power.

My son is gone.
One less vote.

I had two children.
I have two children.

> —Bianca Reynolds
>   Franklin High School
>   Portland, Oregon

WHEN I WAS HIS AGE

My grandma told me
People empty their bladders
When they die
That is how I knew
The boy was dead.

I saw a chunk of his wrist
Gone and blood where a sideburn
Used to be
His uncle
Carried him toward the truck

My temples shouted
Don't you see the urine stain
On his khaki shorts
Old man
It's too late
Mom
There are so many of you
But all they will let you do is
Collapse on the wet ground
And bury your son's body
In a box

And I watch tears
roll down your cheeks.

> —Toyomi Yoshida,
>   Franklin High School
>   Portland, Oregon

NOT US

Thousands dead
His war of greed
No one fed
From his money tree

Roots of red
Wails of despair

Wake up
This isn't our war
We weren't meant to kill
To be numb
To pull the trigger

> —Blake Weber
>   Franklin High School
>   Portland, Oregon

Fahrenheit 9/11:
Thinking in Pictures, Feeling in Words

Suggested Prompts

POETRY SUGGESTIONS:

▪ Start your poem with a line from the film.
▪ Write in the voice of someone from the film: a child, a soldier, a mother.
▪ Write in the voice of an object: a gun, a flag, a microphone.

TWO-VOICE POEM SUGGESTIONS:

▪ Soldier who says, "It's a rush" and soldier who says, "You cannot kill someone without killing a part of yourself."
▪ Lila and the woman protesting the deaths of Iraqi children in D.C.
▪ Lila and a senator whose child is not in the military.
▪ U.S. soldier and Iraqi insurgent.
▪ Flint citizen and corporate executive attending the conference of business people on investing in Iraq.
▪ Military recruiter and peace activist.
▪ Former President Bush and one of the 9/11 families suing the Saudis.

INTERIOR MONOLOGUE AND STORY SUGGESTIONS:

▪ Woman in Iraq after her family's house was bombed: "Where are you, God?"
▪ Soldier at Walter Reed Hospital or going on a night raid.
▪ Soldier who refuses to return to Iraq (Abdul Henderson).
▪ Member of the Congressional Black Caucus as every senator refuses to support their challenge of the election.
▪ The man handcuffed and on the ground during the night sweep.
▪ A military recruiter at the mall in Flint.
▪ Lila when she gets the phone call saying her son is dead.
▪ George W. Bush as he sits in the classroom after hearing about 9/11.
▪ Lila's flag.
▪ One of the bombs that lands in Iraq.

METAPHORICAL DRAWING SUGGESTIONS:

▪ Policymakers behind their masks.
▪ Lila's family as the backbone of American society.
▪ The U.S. public as a confused puppy being given conflicting commands.

CHAPTER 4

Military Recruitment

Early Childhood Military Education?

Formative life lessons begin at a young age

ANN PELO

Does our national security rely on top-quality early childhood education?

Yes, say the military leaders of Mission: Readiness, an organization led by retired military commanders that promotes investment in education, child health, and parenting support. In March, Mission: Readiness released national and state-by-state education briefs, declaring that "high-quality early education is not only important for the children it benefits but also critical to ensuring our military's long-term readiness.... Investing in high-quality early education is a matter of national security."

Actually, the generals are right, but for all the wrong reasons.

They see early childhood education as military readiness training. Mission: Readiness argues that investment in early childhood education for at-risk and low-income children will pay off in higher graduation rates and lower incarceration rates—expanding the pool of potential military recruits. "Recruitment and retention challenges could return if America does not do a better job now of producing more young men and women qualified for service," says the mission statement on the organization's website. "We must ensure America's national security by supporting interventions that will prepare young people for a life of military service and productive citizenship."

> THE GENERALS' AIM IS TO PREPARE LOW-INCOME CHILDREN TO BE SOLDIERS, TRAINED FROM THEIR YOUNGEST YEARS TO FOLLOW DIRECTIONS AND TO COMPLY WITH THE STRICTURES ISSUED BY THE RANKING AUTHORITY.

Who are the young people for whom these military leaders are supposedly advocating? Low-income, at-risk children—the pool of children from which the military has traditionally recruited. What sort of education do the generals want for these children? Skill-and-drill, standards-driven, assessment-burdened curriculum that prepares children for skill-and-drill basic training, for standards-driven military discipline, for test-based military promotion. The generals' aim is to prepare low-income children to be soldiers, trained from their youngest years to follow directions and to comply with the strictures issued by the ranking authority. That's not high-quality education; that's utilitarian education designed to serve military and economic needs.

This approach to education may prepare young people for a life of military service, but it certainly does not prepare them for citizenship. The Mission: Readiness statement of purpose unwittingly exposes a central conundrum in the organization's thinking: "The earliest months and years of life are a crucial time when we build the foundation of children's character, how they relate to others and how they learn."

Exactly. High-quality early childhood education teaches for citizenship, not for test taking and reductionist assessment. The goal is not compliance but creativity, critical thinking, and compassion. Children are invited to engage meaningful questions in collaboration with others, to embrace complexity, to strive for the well-being of others with generosity, to pay attention to issues of fairness, and to act with courage, conviction, and imagination. Top-flight early education fosters in children dispositions toward empathy, ecological consciousness, engaged inquiry, and collaboration. These are the dispositions of citizens.

Citizens care for their country and its security. They inhabit the commons and they act on behalf of the common good. They are emboldened by personal sovereignty and know themselves to be protagonists in the unfolding history of their country—not passive observers, not dull-minded consumers, not obedient followers of military or government direction, but patriots acting for the good of the commonwealth. Active citizens,

thinking critically and compassionately, resist military action as the quick and easy answer to complex challenges. They point out the horrifying absurdity of the idea of "collateral damage." They fight against imperialism and work for justice nationally and internationally.

This is the citizenship that our nation needs at this juncture in our evolution. Wars in Afghanistan and Iraq, a gulf slicked with oil, pristine lands on the chopping block for drilling and mining, health care out of reach for nearly a third of our people, unions under siege by state governments and by corporations—our nation needs citizens concerned with national security, with the well-being of our nation. There is much work to be done, and it will take citizens, not soldiers, to do it.

So, yes, because high-quality early childhood education prepares children to be citizens, it is essential to national security. The investment should and must be a national priority. ■

Ann Pelo (annpelo@msn.com) edited Rethinking Early Childhood Education. *She taught at Hilltop Children's Center in Seattle for 16 years, until 2008.*

MICHAEL DUFFY

The Recruitment Minefield

Today's students live in a kind of parallel universe where they maneuver daily through a psychological minefield of quota-driven recruiters

BILL BIGELOW

E miliano Santiago. Not many of our students know his name. But they should. Santiago joined the Oregon Army National Guard on June 28, 1996, shortly after his high school graduation in Hermiston, Ore. He served honorably, became a sergeant, and was discharged in June 2004, after eight years in the Guard.

But that October, more than three months after his discharge, the government extended Santiago's termination date—to December 24, 2031; yes, 2031; it's not a misprint. Santiago's unit was ordered to report on Jan. 2, 2005, to Fort Sill, Okla., where it would join other soldiers being sent to Afghanistan. Santiago's attorney, Steven Goldberg of the National Lawyers Guild, filed suit in federal court in Portland, arguing that the military had no right to order Santiago to active duty months after he'd been discharged.

During Santiago's hearing, Matthew Lepore, the Justice Department attorney, agreed that Santiago's activation had come after his discharge. But Lepore said that because commanders of Santiago's unit had been told earlier that under the military's stop-loss policy his unit might be mobilized, that was notification enough.

> **IF WE DON'T HELP STUDENTS NURTURE A SKEPTICAL SENSIBILITY ABOUT MILITARY RECRUITMENT AND ENLISTMENT, THEN OUR HIDDEN CURRICULUM IS "DO AS YOU'RE TOLD," "TRUST THE AUTHORITIES," "GOVERNMENT KNOWS BEST."**

True, Lepore acknowledged, Santiago himself was never notified, but that made no difference. Lepore argued that the court was obliged to view this case through a "deferential lens"—to assume the military knew what was best for the military. Judge Owen M. Panner agreed. He ruled against Santiago, saying he believed the military would be harmed more than Santiago if the court ruled against the government. Goldberg appealed to the 9th Circuit Court of Appeals. The court denied the appeal and Santiago was sent to join D Company of the Oregon Guard's 113th Aviation Battalion.

High school teachers, counselors, students, and parents everywhere should know about Santiago's case. Think you're signing up for four years, or eight years? Think again. Santiago was 19 when he entered the military. When his new discharge date rolls around, he'll be 54—if the military doesn't extend it again.

NO CHILD LEFT UNRECRUITED

Thanks to a provision in the No Child Left Behind legislation, military recruiters have easy access to high school students these days. In Portland, where I taught for many years, in 1995 the school board banned organizations that discriminate based on race, sex, or sexual orientation—including the U.S. military—from recruiting in the schools. NCLB overturned that ban, requiring that recruiters have "the same access to secondary school students as is provided generally to post-secondary educational institutions or to prospective employers of those students." The law also requires high schools to provide the military access to students' names, addresses, and telephone numbers—unless a parent or student contacts the school to deny permission to release this information.

It was against the backdrop of the Santiago ruling and increased recruiter access to students that Franklin High School teacher Julie O'Neill began a short unit on military recruitment with her senior political science students. Julie invited me to collaborate on the unit.

We began by asking students to write about their experiences with military recruiters. I was astounded by the students' stories. One hundred percent of O'Neill's students—three untracked classes of almost 40 students each—had been recruited in some manner by one or another branch of the military. Julie's students were typical of the high school as a whole: largely white and working class, with a relatively small number of Asian Americans, Latinos, African Americans, and Native Americans. Recruiters had come into classes ranging from foods ("You have to be in the military to cook for the president, ya know"), to oceanography, to band, to weight training. Recruiters had visited the Latina/o Club, played a key role in the annual field day activities, worked with the student program that links seniors and freshmen, and approached students in the halls.

They'd badgered students in malls, called them repeatedly, emailed them, visited them at home, bought them school supplies, driven them around town, mailed them videos and DVDs, and invited them to mini-boot camp weekends. Even students whose parents had asked the school in writing not to share information with recruiters reported being contacted multiple times. The recruiters' techniques were consistent: find out students' after-graduation aspirations and attempt to convince them that the military was the way to realize these. Channa's story was typical:

My 10th-grade year when I was weight lifting, they asked me, "You ever planned on joining the Marines?" I told them no. He was, like, "You ever thought about having the Marines put you through college?" The Marines called my house at least twice a week. They asked me this year if I ever thought about wrestling for the Marines. I told him no, but he said, "The Marines can help put you through college and pay you to wrestle." One day I was waiting in line to get a bus pass. This Navy guy asked me what I had planned after high school. I told him I might kickbox. He said I could kickbox for the Navy. He handed me his card and walked away.

The Marines have extraordinary access to students in weight training, where they offer a "Marine challenge" curriculum. Recruiters yell at students and give them orders. One student described being in the weight room, "doing a normal workout and all of a sudden three recruiters were at my side counting my reps. I was like, 'WHOAAH!!'"

Cynthia's story showed how recruiters take advantage of the scarcity of college financial aid in their sales pitches:

A few weeks ago a recruiter called me. I wasn't so much annoyed that they were soliciting me as I was disturbed by what the recruiter revealed to me. They asked if I was going to college, and I said, "Yes, I am going to the University of Notre Dame." The recruiter paused, then fired another question. "Wow. That's an expensive school. Do you have money to pay for it?" I replied, "Yes, they are giving me $30,000 every year for four years." Dumbfounded, the officer said, "Well, the Army can offer you lots of experiences that college can't." I told him I wasn't interested, and the conversation ended. Yet I was left with the impression that they prey on kids with either no plans after high school and/or no money to pay for college.

The stories generated grumbling from one or two students. Ben said: "These are so negative. Doesn't anyone have a good story about military recruiters?" But in his own story, Ben wrote about how annoyed he was by recruiters' pressure: "Recruiters are extremely pushy and opinionated. I was promised everything from tuition to guaranteed jobs to free housing."

I read all 100-plus recruitment stories. The more I read, the more overwhelmed I became by the sense that today's students live in a kind of parallel universe where they maneuver daily through a psychological minefield of quota-driven recruiters.

And there was a pattern: Recruiters lie. Claire went with a friend to the recruitment office to take a math test. "When she was done with her test, he told us about how the government pays for you to go to college and after you serve you still get money. I think that was the main reason she wanted to join—that and they told her that she wouldn't have to go to Iraq. How do they know?"

They don't; it was a lie. In "AWOL in America," (Harper's, March 2005), Kathy Dobie reports that the G.I. Rights Hotline has "heard hundreds of stories involving recruiters' lies." As Dobie reports, "One of the most common lies told by recruiters is that it's easy to get out of the military if you change your mind. But once they arrive at training, the recruits are told there's no exit, period—and if you try to leave, you'll be court-martialed and serve 10 years in the brig, you'll never be able to get a good job or a bank loan, and this will follow you around like a felony conviction." It's not true, but as Dobie speculates, the threats are likely effective in keeping some unhappy soldiers from trying to get out. In fact, the expectation that recruiters make promises they can't back up is acknowledged in the enlistment contract that prospective soldiers must sign. More on that extraordinary document later.

FAHRENHEIT 9/11

One of the striking segments in Michael Moore's documentary Fahrenheit 9/11 is the few minutes the film spends with Marine recruiters Staff Sgt. Dale Kortman and Sgt. Raymond Plouhar as they troll for prospects in the Courtland Mall in Flint, Mich. Julie and I showed this segment in class so students could reflect on a number of the techniques that military recruiters employ to snare recruits. Recruiters' choice of the Courtland Mall in Flint instead of the suburban Genesee Valley Mall is emblematic of recruiters' choices around the country: They concentrate on high schools in working-class neighborhoods—like Portland's Franklin High School—but appear less frequently at high schools in more elite neighborhoods.

We showed students the Fahrenheit 9/11 segment to reinforce their own observations that recruiters probe for an individual's career goal and then link that to a future in the military, as in this exchange:

> Sgt. Dale Kortman: Gents! You know we're looking at ya, right! You guys ever thinking about joining up?
>
> John Kingston: I thought about going to college and playing basketball.
>
> Sgt. Kortman: OK, OK. You any good?
>
> Kingston: Yeah. Especially basketball.
>
> Sgt. Kortman: Good. You can play ball for the Marine Corps, as well, you know, travel around the world, get on the Marine Corps basketball team. Um, David Robinson was in the military as well ...
>
> Kingston: Oh, was he?
>
> Sgt. Kortman: So, yeah, so, you can definitely hook it up so.

Never mind that Robinson was in the Navy, not the Marines, went to the elite Naval Academy at Annapolis, and is about seven feet tall. Moore concludes the segment with a poignant comment from a young black man, Martres Brown: "One would love to have that chance to experience college life, you know, stuff young people can do without having the risk of dying in the process."

Students were unfazed, chuckling at the recruiting techniques they recognized. Frankly, I think the segment was more startling to me than to the students. They experience this all the time; I see it in the movies. But it did reinforce our conversations about their recruitment stories. One student remarked, "It seemed the recruiters were hunting their prey." And another: "One of the things I notice is that they target people who have low self-esteem." This may or may not be true, but in discussions students agreed that recruiters seem to concentrate on individuals who do not have the highest grades. Interestingly, students also agreed that young women are more heavily recruited than young men.

Sgt. Plouhar comments to Moore, "It's better to get them when they're ones and twos. And work on them that way." His observation underscores the importance of a critical examination of recruitment practices. Recruiters seek to isolate people in order to "work on them." Anything that promotes questioning is the enemy of recruiters. By contrast, a study of recruitment is best engaged in collectively, as we share stories, look for patterns, patch together insights, and nurture habits of skepticism.

DREAM LIFE OF THE CULTURE

Julie asked students to bring in recruitment brochures, posters, videos, and DVDs that they'd received, so that we could use these to evaluate some of the propaganda techniques used by military recruiters. I'd gone to the local recruitment station to get some more posters and ended up a target of recruitment myself—an all-expense-paid educators' trip to San Diego to learn more about the Marines. The recruiter, Sgt. Héctor Torres, listed all the Portland teachers and counselors who'd taken him up on this offer. "We'll put you up in a nice hotel on the beach." He was sincere, charming, and relentless. I got a taste of how good these guys are.

We taped recruitment posters and brochures around the room at 10 stations, and numbered them with Post-it notes. I introduced the activity by talking a bit about the history of propaganda and advertising. A number of 11th-grade global studies classes at Franklin watch the video *The Ad and the Ego*, probably the best classroom resource on the history of advertising in the United States. I reminded students that *The Ad and the Ego* points out that advertisers' assessment of human motivation has radically shifted since advertising became a major U.S. industry in the 1920s. Then, typical ads were filled with text. Advertisers saw humans as essentially rational beings who, if presented with sufficient evidence, could be convinced to buy their product. Thus an ad for, say, Pepsodent, would include lots of information on the product, why it's good, bad things that could happen if it's not used, and how to use it. But not any longer. Now, advertisers regard individuals as moved more by image and emotion and less by argument.

In the film, University of Massachusetts professor Sut Jhally says: "Advertisers don't really talk about things, they talk about these things [products] in relationship to other things which are important to us. So advertising, I think, is the dream life of the culture, because what it reflects is the things that we really want." Julie and I asked students to pay attention to the deeper appeal in the recruitment materials. We wrote two questions on the board:

What are the dreams that these ads speak to?

What are they trying to "sell" to young people on a deep level?

As a whole class, we practiced on a poster that shows a Marine who appears to be part human and part three-dimensional blueprint—very scientific and machine-like, holding an assault rifle. Students had wonderful insights, finding more dimensions to the ad than I'd considered. They talked about the power that it offers largely powerless high school students, compared it to movies like *The Matrix* and to video games, and pointed out that it promised indestructibility. As one student commented, "It says, 'I can stand up for myself and no one will hurt me.'"

We divided students into 10 groups, and asked each group to go to an assigned poster or brochure displayed around the classroom. We asked them to take notes on the questions we raised and to make additional observations on the materials. After students spent about four or five minutes at one station, we had them move to the next poster and repeated this so that each group viewed and discussed five of the 10 recruitment materials. It was a lively activity, and the students seemed to enjoy peeling back the layers of meaning in the ads.

Afterward, we discussed some of their insights. "This Marine poster is like an invitation to all the weak kids who get picked on: You can defend yourself when you're a Marine. The men are so quick in the picture, it's actually blurred." One of the ads showed young men grimacing as they did pull-ups, with the caption: "Pain is weakness leaving your body." One student commented, "This one is saying that the Marines will help you rise above pain. You can get away from a bad or abusive childhood and get past it."

We followed up by viewing a short promotional video from the National Guard. (These are easy to come by as recruiters hand them out like candy to students.) It promises teamwork—"There is no 'I' in 'team'"—and ticks off all the qualities that someone will acquire or develop in the Guard: loyalty, respect, duty, selfless service, honor, integrity, personal courage, and education. As one student pointed out afterward, "It looks like so much fun, it's not even a job. Like all your dreams can come true. Like summer camp for the government."

THE CONTRACT

It took me weeks to locate a copy of the enlistment contract that recruits sign when entering the military. (See page 112. Also available online: http://usmilitary.about.com/library/pdf/enlistment.pdf) It's a scary document. Ask Emiliano Santiago.

For some of our students, this document will be the most important contract they sign in their entire lives. Joining the military is a life-altering decision, and one that the government urges—indeed bullies—young people to make before they're deemed mature enough even to buy a bottle of beer. A critical examination of this document should be part of the core curriculum in every high school in the United States. It's not hyperbole to say that this study is a matter of life and death.

The "Enlistment/Reenlistment Document—Armed Forces of the United States" is anything but straightforward. In fact, its interpretation was at the center of the Santiago case. In small groups, we distributed colored highlighters to students and asked them to mark passages that they found vague, disturbing, or confusing. We also asked students to circle the four items in the document that they thought were the most important for an individual considering joining the military, and to come up with six questions about the enlistment document.

When we regrouped for discussion, we went page by page. On page 1, Section 8a deals with the delayed entry/enlistment program, which applies to many of our students who join even before they leave high school. Section 8c implicitly acknowledges that some recruiters may have made false promises—like Claire's friend who was told that she wouldn't be sent to Iraq. It reads: "The agreements in this section and attached annex(es) are all the promises made to me by the Government. ANYTHING ELSE ANYONE HAS PROMISED ME IS NOT VALID AND WILL NOT BE HONORED." [Emphasis in original.] Section 8c has a ring of full disclosure, and implies that if a recruit does get something in writing then it will be honored.

Section 9 tells recruits: "Many laws, regulations, and military customs will govern my conduct and require me to do things under this agreement that a civilian does not have to do." The section also states: "I understand that I cannot change these laws but that Congress may change these laws, or pass new laws, at any time that may affect this agreement, and that I will be subject to those laws." Reading this section prompted one student to ask, "How can one sign a contract that is always changing?"

Arguably the most important part of the contract is section 9b—it makes all promises in the document irrelevant:

> Laws and regulations that govern military personnel may change without notice to me. Such changes may affect my status, pay, allowances, benefits, and responsibilities as a member of the Armed Forces REGARDLESS of the provisions of this enlistment/reenlistment document. [emphasis in original]

One student said, "Anything they promise you is BS. Look at it." Another added: "All this needs to say is, 'You're the military's. Sign there.'" Another wondered: "How can the Army focus so much on honor, but not agree to honor agreements?"

As we were teaching this unit, Steven Goldberg, who was Emiliano Santiago's attorney, offered a workshop for Portland teachers during a districtwide inservice day. In a room full of veteran social studies teachers, Goldberg opened: "So, are we at war?" It wasn't merely an academic question. Section 9c says: "In the event of war, my enlistment in the Armed Forces continues until six (6) months after the war ends." So one's length of service in the military turns on the issue of whether the United States is at war. Some teachers argued that Congress has not declared war since 1941; so, no, we're not at war. Others said that President Bush had pronounced a war on terrorism, for which Congress voted funds, so that did constitute "war." And U.S. soldiers are dying in combat in Afghanistan and Iraq, so aren't these wars—in fact, if not in title? If 40 teachers with advanced degrees couldn't agree on such a key question, how could one expect an 18-year-old to interpret this part of the document?

DON'T SIGN UNLESS YOU'RE 100 PERCENT SURE, 100 PERCENT OF THE TIME

Following our examination of the enlistment document, we asked students to offer advice to prospective recruits based on their reading of the enlistment contract. A few pieces of their advice:

Read the contract thoroughly.

Read the Uniform Code of Military Justice.

Don't sign up for the military because you're mad at your parents; you might never see them again.

Take a friend to the recruiters.

Take a lawyer.

Don't sign unless you're 100 percent sure, 100 percent of the time.

Although from the beginning of the unit we'd emphasized that this was not a study of the war, or even of military service, some students naturally had a hard time uncoupling recruitment from military service itself—as revealed in this piece of advice from Jasmina, a young woman who had suffered through war in Bosnia: "Shoot a bird, and then think about whether you can kill a human."

We distributed "Ten Points to Consider Before You Sign a Military Enlistment Agreement" available at afsc.org/content/10-points-enlisting-e. And we asked students to compare the 10 points with the advice they suggested. Many items were similar, including: take a witness when talking with recruiters, carefully read a copy of the enlistment agreement, and don't make a hasty decision when you're upset. To some of us these items might seem like common sense, but these bits of wisdom may be vital as students make key choices about their futures.

PHONY MEMO

In class, we had not yet talked about the Santiago case. Julie had a brilliant idea to introduce it. She drafted a phony memo from the principal full of dire language: "Early data indicate that Franklin is falling far behind projected goals and is in danger of being labeled a failing school under No Child Left Behind. Thus, Franklin's school year will be extended an extra month and graduation will be postponed to June 30. I apologize for any inconvenience this may cause, but take comfort in the shared vision of Portland Public Schools and Franklin High School to educate all its children." It was pitch perfect memo-speak. Julie put it on the principal's letterhead (with permission), used his signature stamp, and asked a colleague, Jim Dyal, to feign agitation and deliver the document to her. When he arrived at the door, Julie pretended that she was too busy to deal with it and when Dyal persisted, she asked a student to read it aloud to the class.

Students bought the charade and were dumbfounded. I took notes as they voiced their anger at this month-long extension of their school year:

"They can't do that, I have plans."

"Can I sue for the plane ticket I bought?"

"Let's walk out. Who's down?"

"That's not fair. We've had to make plans for the summer. Can they legally do that?"

It was only when Julie put a transparency of the "memo" on the overhead and asked students to list their arguments against graduation postponement that they realized it was a hoax.

Then we distributed an article on the Santiago case. His enlistment had been extended 27 years. Their school year had been—momentarily—extended 27 days. Julie wanted to give students a small dose of what it would feel like to have one's expectation of freedom ruptured. A number of students were a bit sheepish when they compared their outrage at a delayed graduation with how Santiago must feel as he faces a much greater, and more perilous, delay in his discharge.

We wanted students to understand the government's argument in the Santiago case, as it's a position that anyone considering enlistment should be aware of. Steven Goldberg had faxed us a part of the U.S. government's brief defending its cancellation of Santiago's discharge. It is grounded in the government's interpretation of the contract between the government and an enlistee. Here's a key passage from the brief filed with the 9th Circuit Court of Appeals:

> Enlistment in the armed forces does not constitute merely a bargain between two parties, but effects a change of status by which "the citizen becomes a soldier": "no breach of the contract destroys the new status or relieves …the obligations which its existence imposes." Bell v. United States, 366 U.S. 393, 402 (1961), quoting In re Grimley, 17 U.S. 147, 151-152 (1890).

In other words, it doesn't make any difference if the government violated the enlistment agreement with Santiago regarding his date of release from military service. Once he signed that contract, he no longer was merely a citizen but was a soldier, and when you're a soldier you're subject to military rule and laws governing the military.

ADVERTISING THE TRUTH

For the final assignment in the unit, Julie asked students to design truth-in-advertising pieces about military enlistment. Each had to have a specific target audience and include a clear message drawing on something we studied in class. The ads needed to be visually effective, publishable, provide sources—and truthful.

A number of students patterned their alternative ads on actual military recruitment ads or brochures and downloaded images from military websites. Many looked professional and had to be read to recognize the satire, as in Garrett Ross's ad for the U.S. Army Reserves:

> When it comes to strength and security...no, no, don't bother reading that fine print. It's just legal gibberish. Just sign there. Don't worry, we'll take care of this stuff. We've got lawyers and crap like that. Y'ever shoot a gun, kid? It's really cool.

Emily Beloof's brochure kept the Army's original language on the cover:

> There is another girl inside of you. When you wanted to stop, she pushed you harder. When you needed rest, she ran farther. She knows no bounds and tests all of the limits. She is stronger than you allow yourself to be. There is a girl inside of you who always wanted to run with the big dogs. She will not settle until she has become the best she can be. There is another girl inside you.

Open the brochure, and Emily's text takes a deeper look at "the girl inside of you":

> Can she go the distance when her orders contradict her morals or ethics or what she knows to be right and good? Is she willing to live with broken promises? The Army can change your contract at any time without your permission. Be aware. Know what you do when you join up. The girl inside you needs your direction. When she considers the military, make sure you ask a few questions.

On the Internet, Jessica Killops found a startling image by Charles Moffat of a woman being gagged by a U.S. flag. She incorporated this into a poster denouncing militarism as an attack on women. Without a doubt, Jessica's statistics that 90 percent of recent women veterans had experienced sexual harassment of some kind in the military, and almost one-third of these reported being raped, sent shock waves through the classroom.

COMBATTING A CURRICULUM OF IGNORANCE

This was a first-time effort for both of us, so there are some things we would do differently. Ultimately, the fullest evaluation of military service needs to be grounded in an examination of what the military is actually doing. There are essential critical tools students can develop from a unit like this, but it would be more powerful were it connected to a broader look at the role of the U.S. military in the world, particularly in Afghanistan and Iraq. In fact, in our final activity,

asking students to discuss their alternative ads in small groups, the discussions that I heard centered on why the United States is involved in Iraq. What's on students' minds is not just recruitment, but the military itself and the Iraq war.

As implied in Ben's earlier comment about wanting to hear a "good story" about military service, a few students thought that by raising questions about the military we were beating up on the United States. They worried that we were attacking decisions that their family members had made, or even challenging their future career choices. These students thought we should have featured stories of vets who had enjoyed and benefited from their service. I can understand how our critical stance could have felt "one-sided" to some students. But our aim was not "balance." This was not a unit on "here's some bad stuff about the military and here's some good stuff." During their senior year of high school, students are massively assaulted by military propaganda. Much is dishonest, much is manipulative. Helping students develop the capacity to question recruitment materials could literally save someone's life. That's what we were after.

If we don't help students nurture this skeptical sensibility about military recruitment and enlistment, then our hidden curriculum is "Do as you're told," "Trust the authorities," "Government knows best." This is profoundly undemocratic. It's a curriculum of ignorance. How we teach about vital issues like recruitment says something about the kind of world we want to help create: Do we want people to be active, questioning, and engaged, or simply to be consumers of other people's plans?

In a segment of PBS' *News Hour with Jim Lehrer*, Emiliano Santiago's mother said that as a high school junior Santiago had been "lured by the uniform of the recruiters." How students react to the lure of the uniform, finding "the other girl inside you," or any other recruitment ploy depends, in part, on our curriculum. We owe it to our students to help them critically evaluate the hard-sell and the lavish promises. ▪

ENLISTMENT/REENLISTMENT DOCUMENT
ARMED FORCES OF THE UNITED STATES

PRIVACY ACT STATEMENT

AUTHORITY: 5 U.S.C. 3331; 10 U.S.C. 113, 136, 502, 504, 505, 506, 507, 508, 509, 510, 513, 515, 516, 518, 519, 972, 978, 2107, 2107a, 3253, 3258, 3262, 5540, 8252, 8253, 8257, 8258, 12102, 12103, 12104, 12105, 12106, 12107, 12108, 12301, 12302, 12304, 12305, 12405; 14 USC 351, 632; 32 U.S.C. 301, 302, 303, 304; and Executive Order 9397, November 1943 (SSN).

PRINCIPAL PURPOSE(S): To record enlistment or reenlistment into the U.S. Armed Forces. This information becomes a part of the subject's military personnel records which are used to document promotion, reassignment, training, medical support, and other personnel management actions. The purpose of soliciting the SSN is for positive identification.

ROUTINE USE(S): This form becomes a part of the Service's Enlisted Master File and Field Personnel File. All uses of the form are internal to the relevant Service.

DISCLOSURE: Voluntary; however, failure to furnish personal identification information may negate the enlistment/reenlistment application.

A. ENLISTEE/REENLISTEE IDENTIFICATION DATA

1. NAME *(Last, First, Middle)*

2. SOCIAL SECURITY NUMBER

3. HOME OF RECORD *(Street, City, County, State, Country, ZIP Code)*

4. PLACE OF ENLISTMENT/REENLISTMENT *(Mil. Installation, City, State)*

5. DATE OF ENLISTMENT/ REENLISTMENT *(YYYYMMDD)*

6. DATE OF BIRTH *(YYYYMMDD)*

7. PREV MIL SVC UPON ENL/REENLIST	YEARS	MONTHS	DAYS
a. TOTAL ACTIVE MILITARY SERVICE			
b. TOTAL INACTIVE MILITARY SERVICE			

B. AGREEMENTS

8. I am enlisting/reenlisting in the United States *(list branch of service)* _____ this date for _____ years and _____ weeks beginning in pay grade _____ of which _____ years and _____ weeks is considered an Active Duty Obligation, and _____ years and _____ weeks will be served in the Reserve Component of the Service in which I have enlisted. If this is an initial enlistment, I must serve a total of eight (8) years, unless I am sooner discharged or otherwise extended by the appropriate authority. This eight year service requirement is called the Military Service Obligation. The additional details of my enlistment/ reenlistment are in Section C and Annex(es) *(list name of Annex(es) and describe)*

_____

_____

a. FOR ENLISTMENT IN A DELAYED ENTRY/ENLISTMENT PROGRAM (DEP):
I understand that I am joining the DEP. I understand that by joining the DEP I am enlisting in the Ready Reserve component of the United States *(list branch of service)* _____ for a period not to exceed 365 days, unless this period of time is otherwise extended by the Secretary concerned. While in the DEP, I understand that I am in a nonpay status and that I am not entitled to any benefits or privileges as a member of the Ready Reserve, to include, but not limited to medical care, liability insurance, death benefits, education benefits, or disability retired pay if I incur a physical disability. I understand that the period of time while I am in the DEP is NOT creditable for pay purposes upon entry into a pay status. However, I also understand that the period of time while I am in the DEP is counted toward fulfillment of my military service obligation described in paragraph 10, below. While in the DEP, I understand that I must maintain my current qualifications and keep my recruiter informed of any changes in my physical or dependency status, qualifications, and mailing address. I understand that I WILL be ordered to active duty unless I report to the place shown in item 4 above by *(list date (YYYYMMDD))* _____ for enlistment in the Regular component of the United States *(list branch of service)* _____ for not less than _____ years and _____ weeks.

b. REMARKS: *(If none, so state.)*

c. The agreements in this section and attached annex(es) are all the promises made to me by the Government. **ANYTHING ELSE ANYONE HAS PROMISED ME IS NOT VALID AND WILL NOT BE HONORED.**
(Initials of Enlistee/Reenlistee) _____

(Continued on Page 2)

DD FORM 4/1, OCT 2007   PREVIOUS EDITION IS OBSOLETE.   Adobe Professional 8.0

C. PARTIAL STATEMENT OF EXISTING UNITED STATES LAWS

9. FOR ALL ENLISTEES OR REENLISTEES:
I understand that many laws, regulations, and military customs will govern my conduct and require me to do things under this agreement that a civilian does not have to do. I also understand that various laws, some of which are listed in this agreement, directly affect this enlistment/reenlistment agreement. Some examples of how existing laws may affect this agreement are explained in paragraphs 10 and 11. I understand that I cannot change these laws but that Congress may change these laws, or pass new laws, at any time that may affect this agreement, and that I will be subject to those laws and any changes they make to this agreement. I further understand that:

a. My enlistment/reenlistment agreement is more than an employment agreement. It effects a change in status from civilian to military member of the Armed Forces. As a member of the Armed Forces of the United States, I will be:

(1) Required to obey all lawful orders and perform all assigned duties.

(2) Subject to separation during or at the end of my enlistment. If my behavior fails to meet acceptable military standards, I may be discharged and given a certificate for less than honorable service, which may hurt my future job opportunities and my claim for veteran's benefits.

(3) Subject to the military justice system, which means, among other things, that I may be tried by military courts-martial.

(4) Required upon order to serve in combat or other hazardous situations.

(5) Entitled to receive pay, allowances, and other benefits as provided by law and regulation.

b. Laws and regulations that govern military personnel may change without notice to me. Such changes may affect my status, pay, allowances, benefits, and responsibilities as a member of the Armed Forces **REGARDLESS** of the provisions of this enlistment/reenlistment document.

10. MILITARY SERVICE OBLIGATION, SERVICE ON ACTIVE DUTY AND STOP-LOSS FOR ALL MEMBERS OF THE ACTIVE AND RESERVE COMPONENTS, INCLUDING THE NATIONAL GUARD.

a. FOR ALL ENLISTEES: If this is my initial enlistment, I must serve a total of eight (8) years, unless I am sooner discharged or otherwise extended by the appropriate authority. This eight year service requirement is called the Military Service Obligation. Any part of that service not served on active duty must be served in the Reserve Component of the service in which I have enlisted. If this is a reenlistment, I must serve the number of years specified in this agreement, unless I am sooner discharged or otherwise extended by the appropriate authority. Some laws that affect when I may be ordered to serve on active duty, the length of my service on active duty, and the length of my service in the Reserve Component, even beyond the eight years of my Military Service Obligation, are discussed in the following paragraphs.

b. I understand that I can be ordered to active duty at any time while I am a member of the DEP. In a time of war, my enlistment may be extended without my consent for the duration of the war and for six months after its end (10 U.S.C. 506, 12103(c)).

c. As a member of a Reserve Component of an Armed Force, in time of war or of national emergency declared by the Congress, I may, without my consent, be ordered to serve on active duty, for the entire period of the war or emergency and for six (6) months after its end (10 U.S.C. 12301(a)). My enlistment may be extended during this period without my consent (10 U.S.C. 12103(c)).

d. As a member of the Ready Reserve (to include Delayed Entry Program), in time of national emergency declared by the President, I may, without my consent, be ordered to serve on active duty, and my military service may be extended without my consent, for not more than 24 consecutive months (10 U.S.C. 12302). My enlistment may be extended during this period without my consent (see paragraph 10g).

e. As a member of the Ready Reserve, I may, at any time and without my consent, be ordered to active duty to complete a total of 24 months of active duty, and my enlistment may be extended so I can complete the total of 24 months of active duty, if:

(1) I am not assigned to, or participating unsatisfactorily in, a unit of the Ready Reserve; and

(2) I have not met my Reserve obligation; and

(3) I have not served on active duty for a total of 24 months (10 U.S.C. 12303).

f. As a member of the Selected Reserve or as a member of the Individual Ready Reserve mobilization category, when the President determines that it is necessary to augment the active forces for any operational mission or for certain emergencies, I may, without my consent, be ordered to active duty for not more than 365 days (10 U.S.C. 12304). My enlistment may be extended during this period without my consent (see paragraph 10g).

g. During any period members of a Reserve component are serving on active duty pursuant to an order to active duty under authority of 10 U.S.C. 12301, 12302, or 12304, the President may suspend any provision of law relating to my promotion, retirement, or separation from the Armed Forces if he or his designee determines I am essential to the national security of the United States. Such an action may result in an extension, without my consent, of the length of service specified in this agreement. Such an extension is often called a "stop-loss" extension (10 U.S.C. 12305).

h. I may, without my consent, be ordered to perform additional active duty training for not more than 45 days if I have not fulfilled my military service obligation and fail in any year to perform the required training duty satisfactorily. If the failure occurs during the last year of my required membership in the Ready Reserves, my enlistment may be extended until I perform that additional duty, but not for more than six months (10 U.S.C. 10148).

11. FOR ENLISTEES/REENLISTEES IN THE NAVY, MARINE CORPS, OR COAST GUARD: I understand that if I am serving on a naval vessel in foreign waters, and my enlistment expires, I will be returned to the United States for discharge as soon as possible consistent with my desires. However, if essential to the public interest, I understand that I may be retained on active duty until the vessel returns to the United States. If I am retained under these circumstances, I understand I will be discharged not later than 30 days after my return to the United States; and, that except in time of war, I will be entitled to an increase in basic pay of 25 percent from the date my enlistment expires to the date of my discharge.

12. FOR ALL MALE APPLICANTS: Completion of this form constitutes registration with the Selective Service System in accordance with the Military Selective Service Act. Incident thereto the Department of Defense may transmit my name, permanent address, military address, Social Security Number, and birthdate to the Selective Service System for recording as evidence of the registration.

(Initials of Enlistee/Reenlistee) _____

DD FORM 4/1 (PAGE 2), OCT 2007

NAME OF ENLISTEE/REENLISTEE *(Last, First, Middle)*	SOCIAL SECURITY NO. OF ENLISTEE/REENLISTEE

D. CERTIFICATION AND ACCEPTANCE

13a. My acceptance for enlistment is based on the information I have given in my application for enlistment. If any of that information is false or incorrect, this enlistment may be voided or terminated administratively by the Government or I may be tried by a Federal, civilian, or military court and, if found guilty, may be punished.

I certify that I have carefully read this document, including the partial statement of existing United States laws in Section C and how they may affect this agreement. Any questions I had were explained to my satisfaction. I fully understand that only those agreements in Section B and Section C of this document or recorded on the attached annex(es) will be honored. I also understand that any other promises or guarantees made to me by anyone that are not set forth in Section B or the attached annex(es) are not effective and will not be honored.

b. SIGNATURE OF ENLISTEE/REENLISTEE	c. DATE SIGNED *(YYYYMMDD)*

14. SERVICE REPRESENTATIVE CERTIFICATION

a. On behalf of the United States *(list branch of service)* _____ ,
I accept this applicant for enlistment. I have witnessed the signature in item 13b to this document. I certify that I have explained that only those agreements in Section B of this form and in the attached Annex(es) will be honored, and any other promises made by any person are not effective and will not be honored.

b. NAME *(Last, First, Middle)*	c. PAY GRADE	d. UNIT/COMMAND NAME
e. SIGNATURE	f. DATE SIGNED *(YYYYMMDD)*	g. UNIT/COMMAND ADDRESS *(City, State, ZIP Code)*

E. CONFIRMATION OF ENLISTMENT OR REENLISTMENT

15. IN THE ARMED FORCES EXCEPT THE NATIONAL GUARD (ARMY OR AIR):
   I, _____ , do solemnly swear (or affirm) that I will support and defend the Constitution of the United States against all enemies, foreign and domestic; that I will bear true faith and allegiance to the same; and that I will obey the orders of the President of the United States and the orders of the officers appointed over me, according to regulations and the Uniform Code of Military Justice. So help me God.

16. IN THE NATIONAL GUARD (ARMY OR AIR):
   I, _____ , do solemnly swear (or affirm) that I will support and defend the Constitution of the United States and the State of _____ against all enemies, foreign and domestic; that I will bear true faith and allegiance to the same; and that I will obey the orders of the President of the United States and the Governor of _____ and the orders of the officers appointed over me, according to law and regulations. So help me God.

17. IN THE NATIONAL GUARD (ARMY OR AIR):
   I do hereby acknowledge to have voluntarily enlisted/reenlisted this _____ day of _____ , _____ in the _____ National Guard and as a Reserve of the United States *(list branch of service)* _____ with membership in the _____ National Guard of the United States for a period of _____ years, _____ months, _____ days, under the conditions prescribed by law, unless sooner discharged by proper authority.

18.a. SIGNATURE OF ENLISTEE/REENLISTEE	b. DATE SIGNED *(YYYYMMDD)*

19. ENLISTMENT/REENLISTMENT OFFICER CERTIFICATION
   a. The above oath was administered, subscribed, and duly sworn to (or affirmed) before me this date.

b. NAME *(Last, First, Middle)*	c. PAY GRADE	d. UNIT/COMMAND NAME
e. SIGNATURE	f. DATE SIGNED *(YYYYMMDD)*	g. UNIT/COMMAND ADDRESS *(City, State, ZIP Code)*

(Initials of Enlistee/Reenlistee) _____

DD FORM 4/2, OCT 2007   PREVIOUS EDITION IS OBSOLETE.

NAME OF ENLISTEE/REENLISTEE *(Last, First, Middle)*	SOCIAL SECURITY NO. OF ENLISTEE/REENLISTEE

F. DISCHARGE FROM/DELAYED ENTRY/ENLISTMENT PROGRAM

20a. I request to be discharged from the Delayed Entry/Enlistment Program (DEP) and enlisted in the Regular Component of the

United States *(list branch of service)* _____ for a period of _____ years and

_____ weeks. No changes have been made to my enlistment options OR if changes were made they are recorded on

Annex(es) _____

_____

which replace(s) Annex(es) _____

_____ .

b. SIGNATURE OF DELAYED ENTRY/ENLISTMENT PROGRAM ENLISTEE	**c. DATE SIGNED** *(YYYYMMDD)*

G. APPROVAL AND ACCEPTANCE BY SERVICE REPRESENTATIVE

21. SERVICE REPRESENTATIVE CERTIFICATION

a. This enlistee is discharged from the Reserve Component shown in item 8 and is accepted for enlistment in the Regular

Component of the United States *(list branch of service)* _____ in pay grade _____ .

b. NAME *(Last, First, Middle)*	**c. PAY GRADE**	**d. UNIT/COMMAND NAME**
e. SIGNATURE	**f. DATE SIGNED** *(YYYYMMDD)*	**g. UNIT/COMMAND ADDRESS** *(City, State, ZIP Code)*

H. CONFIRMATION OF ENLISTMENT OR REENLISTMENT

22a. IN A REGULAR COMPONENT OF THE ARMED FORCES:

I, _____ , do solemnly swear (or affirm) that I will support and defend

the Constitution of the United States against all enemies, foreign and domestic; that I will bear true faith and allegiance to the same;

and that I will obey the orders of the President of the United States and the orders of the officers appointed over me, according to

regulations and the Uniform Code of Military Justice. So help me God.

b. SIGNATURE OF ENLISTEE/REENLISTEE	**c. DATE SIGNED** *(YYYYMMDD)*

23. ENLISTMENT OFFICER CERTIFICATION

a. The above oath was administered, subscribed, and duly sworn to (or affirmed) before me this date.

b. NAME *(Last, First, Middle)*	**c. PAY GRADE**	**d. UNIT/COMMAND NAME**
e. SIGNATURE	**f. DATE SIGNED** *(YYYYMMDD)*	**g. UNIT/COMMAND ADDRESS** *(City, State, ZIP Code)*

(Initials of Enlistee/Reenlistee) _____

DD FORM 4/3, OCT 2007   PREVIOUS EDITION IS OBSOLETE.   [Reset]

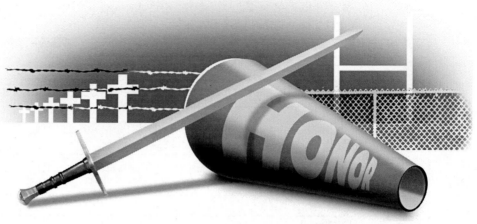

MICHAEL DUFFY

War Is Fun as Hell

The military goes to extraordinary lengths to find recruits

SHELDON RAMPTON
RETHINKING SCHOOLS (Summer 2006)

Years of writing about public relations and propaganda has probably made me a bit jaded, but I was amazed nevertheless when I visited America's Army, an online video game website sponsored by the U.S. Department of Defense (DoD). In its quest to find recruits, the military has literally turned war into entertainment.

America's Army offers a range of games that kids can download or play online. Although the games are violent, with plenty of opportunities to shoot and blow things up, they avoid graphic images of death or other ugliness of war. Instead, they offer a sanitized, Tom Clancy version of fantasy combat. One game, Overmatch, promises "a contest in which one opponent is distinctly superior ... with specialized skills and superior technology." At one point it defines Overmatch as "few soldiers, certain victory" (more or less the same overconfident message that helped lead us into Iraq).

> **IN ITS QUEST TO FIND RECRUITS, THE MILITARY HAS LITERALLY TURNED WAR INTO ENTERTAINMENT.**

Ubisoft, the company contracted to develop the DoD's games, also sponsors the "Frag Dolls," a real-world group of attractive, young women gamers who go by names such as "Eekers," "Valkyrie" and "Jinx" and are paid to promote Ubisoft products. At a computer gaming conference, the Frag Dolls were deployed as booth babes at the America's Army demo, where they played the game and posed for photos and video). On the Frag Dolls weblog, Eekers described her turn at the Combat Convoy experience:

You have this gigantic Hummer in a tent loaded with guns, a rotatable turret, and a huge screen in front of it. Jinx took the wheel and drove us around this virtual war zone while shooting people with a pistol, and I switched off from the SAW turret on the top of the vehicle to riding passenger with an M4.

TIPS FOR RECRUITERS

Military officials have developed an elaborate public relations strategy for outreach to schools. In fall 2004, the Army published a guidebook for high school recruiters. Specific advice includes the following:

Be so helpful and so much a part of the school scene that you are in constant demand.

Cultivate coaches, librarians, administrative staff and teachers.

Know your student influencers. Students such as class officers, newspaper and yearbook editors, and athletes can help build interest in the Army among the student body.

Distribute desk calendars to your assigned schools.

Attend athletic events at the high school. Make sure you wear your uniform.

Get involved with the parent-teacher association.

Coordinate with school officials to eat lunch in the school cafeteria several times each month.

Deliver donuts and coffee for the faculty once a month.

Coordinate with the homecoming committee to get involved with the parade.

Get involved with the local Boy Scouts. . . . Many scouts are high school students and potential enlistees or student influencers.

Order personal presentation items (pens, bags, mouse pads, mugs) as needed monthly for special events.

Attend as many school holiday functions or assemblies as possible.

Offer to be a timekeeper at football games.

Wear your dress blues and participate in school events.

Contact the high school athletic director and arrange for an exhibition basketball game between the faculty and Army recruiters.

GRAND THEFT PRIVACY

The *Washington Post* reported that the Pentagon contracted with BeNOW, a private database marketing company, to "create a database of high school students ages 16 to 18 and all college students to help the military identify potential recruits." The new database is described on the Pentagon database as "arguably the largest repository of 16-to-25-year-old youth data in the country, containing roughly 30 million records."

According to the military's *Federal Register* notice, the information kept on each person includes name, gender, address, birthday, email address, ethnicity, telephone number, high school, college, graduation dates, grade-point average, education level, and military test scores.

Privacy rights groups have been sharply critical of the database. According to a joint statement by a coalition of eight privacy groups, the database violates the Privacy Act, a law intended to reduce government collection of personal data on Americans. The database plan, they wrote, "proposes to ignore the law and its own regulations by collecting personal information from commercial data brokers and state registries rather than directly from individuals." ■

Sheldon Rampton is the coauthor of Weapons of Mass Deception: The Uses of Propaganda in Bush's War on Iraq. *A longer version of this article was written for the Center for Media & Democracy and is available online at www.prwatch.org/node/3865.*

The Next Generation of Soldiers

When Eliza Leas wrote this article, she was in the 8th grade and living in South Burlington, Vt.

ELIZA LEAS

On Friday, June 10, 2005, I entered the cafeteria in Frederick H. Tuttle Middle School in South Burlington, Vt., only to be greeted by a strange sight. A large screen had been set up on the stage, and adults were milling around and passing out flyers. I glanced down at a flyer on the nearest table and was indignant to find that this invasion of my middle school's cafeteria had been orchestrated by none other than the police and the Vermont National Guard.

The point of the presentation was to encourage middle school students to attend a camp that is designed to keep kids "off the streets." A movie began to play on the screen, and other students and I walked closer, curious. I was repelled by what I saw: kids my age doing jumping jacks in army-style pants. Why would normal "campers" be walking around in Army attire?

I am 12 years old. I will not be eligible to be in the armed services for another six years. So why do they insist on advertising in my middle school? I can barely tolerate that they are in my sister's high school lobby every day. Now they're trying to recruit me and other kids, barely out of childhood. I said something to my friend along the lines of "This is so stupid, I don't want to be recruited!" A policeman standing nearby immediately latched on. He tried to convince me and my friend that the presentation wasn't about recruitment and that I shouldn't judge the camp before going and finding out what it's really about. He asked sarcastically, "Do you even understand the concept of a camp?"

YOU CAN ALWAYS TELL A WAR HAS GONE BAD WHEN THE GOVERNMENT STARTS TARGETING CHILDREN IN ITS SEARCH FOR SOLDIERS.

Is the Guard trying to justify its revolting recruiting tactics by saying that they are coming to schools to "help prevent crime"? If the purpose of the camp is to prevent crime, why are the campers engaging in activities such as "security patrol" and "land navigation training"? Perhaps the answer to all my questions lies in a simple statistic: The Army hasn't met its recruitment goals for the fourth month in a row, and it's becoming desperate. Now the armed forces are trying to recruit and train younger and younger kids.

You can always tell a war has gone bad when the government starts targeting children in its search for soldiers. It has to stop, and soon. It has to stop before one more Iraqi child is killed. Before one more American dies in a pointless and unjust war that is supposed to be over, while we keep sending troops. It has to stop before one more human life winks out because cruel warmongers were put into power. It just has to stop.

CHAPTER 5

Antiwar Resistance

TV Selfishness and Violence Explode During 'War on Terror'

2nd graders discover new trends in TV since 9/11

MARGOT PEPPER
RETHINKING SCHOOLS (Spring 2008)

Six years into the "War on Terror," my 2nd-grade Spanish immersion students found that aggression, selfishness, and insults have exploded on national television.

For the last decade, I've had my students at Rosa Parks Elementary School in Berkeley, Calif., analyze television shows preceding National TV-Off week, organized by the TV-Turnoff Network. I ask the 7- and 8-year-old students to collect all the data themselves. For seven days, students study a random sampling of about 35 English and Spanish-language children's television shows—and one or two soap operas or reality shows.

The first day of the study, as homework, students shade in a square on a special graph sheet each time they see hitting, hurting, or killing on half-hour segments of the shows they regularly watch, viewed from beginning to end. The second day, they focus on acts of selfishness; the third day, on instances of put-downs; and the fourth day, on the number of times a typical class rule is broken. Finally, in class, four groups of students compile the data produced by the homework, each focusing on one of the four variables in the study. But in April 2007, when I pulled out model graphs compiled by a class in April 2002—year one of President Bush's war on terror—the contrasts between their graphs and those produced five years prior shocked my students.

"In a half hour of [the cartoon] *Jackie Chan* in 2002 you would see hitting 10 times at most," wrote 7-year-old Flynn Michael-Legg in the essay I assigned summarizing the findings of our study. "In 2007, shows of *Jackie Chan* had [up to] 34 hitting scenes." For the 2001-02 season, nearly one-fourth of the television shows my students watched had one or no acts of violence at all in one half-hour. Now of the shows they watch, only *That's So Raven* continues to have no violence, and all other shows have at least three instances of hitting or violence in one half-hour. Today, nearly half the shows randomly viewed by my students contain seven to 34 instances of hitting or other violent acts each half-hour.

The maximum number of put-downs or insults has nearly doubled since 2002, going from 10 in *That's So Raven* to 18 in *Dumb and Dumber*—over one put-down every two minutes. In *SpongeBob SquarePants*, Flynn pointed out, one would hear at most two put-downs in 2002. Today it's 16. No shows had more than 10 put-downs in 2002. Now three shows did—*SpongeBob*: 16; *Dumb and*

Dumber: 18; *Betty la fea*: 13. Very few shows have no insults at all any more.

All the shows my students watched in 2007 showed people or characters being selfish at least once per half-hour segment. From our class rule to "be considerate and cooperative," my students interpreted "selfish" to mean any time a character did something that put him- or herself first at the expense of someone else. In 2002, only three shows had more than three acts of selfishness in a half-hour. Now, 10 did. Half of the 2007 shows contained five to nine instances of selfishness in each episode.

Students also found that in April 2002, only one show depicted the violation of ordinary class rules—making good decisions: no hitting, put-downs, being unsafe, etc.—12 or more times. In April 2007, the number of such programs rose to six. In 2002, the maximum times class rules were broken on a given half-hour show was 17. In 2007 the number of such shows quadrupled with the maximum number of rules broken on a given show doubling or reaching over 35. The worst offenders, with 18 or more broken rules, were *SpongeBob, Dumb and Dumber, Jackie Chan*, and *Phil of the Future*—the latter two topping the hitting and selfishness categories as well.

THE TV IN OUR HEADS

Whenever students exhibit disruptive behavior, appearing to ape television—pretend shooting, arms flailing, mouth ceaselessly chattering gibberish, etc.—I ask them to please turn off the television in their head if they happen to have left it running. Students often chuckle and, following my lead, turn off an imaginary knob around their ear. Now, as we embarked on our study, many of these students seemed eager to learn more about the television implants I implied existed in their brains; others appeared enchanted with the excuse to watch the boob tube as homework. (Every year, one or two students are excused from the homework due to parental objections to television viewing or, like their teacher, the absence of a set at home. They serve as positive role models and still participate in the class data analysis.)

After sorting the completed television homework graphs into four piles, I assigned one variable (e.g., violence) to student groups to compile into one of four large rainbow-colored graphs like the 2001–02 model I put on the board.

"Which homework graph sheet recorded the highest number of hitting or hurting instances?" I asked the "blue group" in Spanish. Students sifted through to find the greatest number of shaded-in squares.

"¡Mira! ¡*Jackie Chan* tiene 34!" (Look! *Jackie Chan* has 34!) Leah Abramsom voiced her discovery in perfect Spanish, though her multi-ethnic roots, which include African American and Jewish, do not include Latina.

For the sake of easy comparison, I wrote "*Jackie Chan*" on our Violence Graph in the same color and position as it appeared on the 2002 graph. Then I had a student color in 34 squares.

"Let's put a check by every *Jackie Chan* you see on other homework sheets because we're done looking at that program," I reminded them. "Now which homework has the next largest number to 34 of violent acts?"

Just as my students had in 2002, the students proceeded to record the top 16 most violent shows they had seen, assigning each a particular color. After each group of five students completed its bar graph of findings, and they saw it next to the 2002 graph for the same variable, they were visibly horrified. Gisell González clasped hands over her mouth to refrain from completing an exclamation of "Oh my," while others gasped, "Ieeew!"

WHAT DO THE EXPERTS SAY?

Ever since the first month of school when we studied opposing points of view about the so-called discovery (or not) of the Americas, I encouraged my students to turn to other sources like library books and the internet to answer questions, prove social studies and science hypotheses, and, for the most skilled, to question the sources of their answers. So when I proposed searching the internet to support our findings, many were delighted.

The next day, I rotated each group of five through my English internet research station around a large computer. The class had decided on the preliminary Google search terms: "television violence increase." Though students controlled the mouse and keyboard, I helped weed out irrelevant sites and urged them to explore promising ones. We scrolled through these until we found something that either the students or I thought related to our hypothesis about increased violence. Next, I gave them time to read paragraphs on the screen to each other. "Puppies" (native English speakers) read the material to the "kittens" (English language learners), explaining if necessary. When they got to a finding, they would let me know so I could record it on chart paper in the color corresponding to their group.

Traditionally, in this way, virtually all students have been able to discover something to share with their group. Usually two students in each group alight on juicy, complex information and, perhaps because of the immersion program's need for translation, are able to simplify explanations for the rest. The overall quality of research and writing vocabulary has been extraordinary in part because of each group's heterogeneous composition ranging from one to two high-skilled students to one or two who are currently performing well below grade level. Typically, my two-way Spanish immersion classes have been composed of one third children of college-educated professionals; half qualify for free lunches. About a third are native Spanish speakers or Latina/o children; up to one-fifth African American children, and the rest Euro-American and other minorities.

I had the "green group" explore the TV-Turnoff Network site. The students clicked on the Real Vision study. "Wow! Kids will have seen '200,000 violent acts on television by age 18 ... and 16,000 murders,'" Maeve Gallagher read in a shocked voice. Some wondered if the increase in television violence highlighted on the site had led to more real-life killing.

"What words do you think you might see in a report that says killing is related to television?"

They decided on "television + violence + killing."

"Oh my gosh! 'TV shows and Video Games Teach Children to Kill!' Look, down there!" Ceilidh Welsh was pointing to the screen of search results. The note turned out to be a footnote in a report from the Parents Television Council (PTC). I showed the group how important it was to trace primary sources and helped them type in the name of the author of the study, which turned up in a Senate judiciary report.

"This is a report by our own government!" Now I was excited, too. We typed in the report's title and got the full report entitled "Children, Violence, and the Media."

"Video Games and TV are 'teaching kids to kill' and 'teaching them to like it!'" Maeve read aloud for us from the report.

"Violence on TV is over 300 times more than before the war!" Students in the subsequent yellow group were jumping up and down. Well, not exactly. I darted to the board and shaded parts of pizzas to explain percentages. This made the concept more understandable to some, but for most, I had to translate. Using both the internet and fact sheets, children in the "yellow group" found that according to a 2007 study by the PTC called

"Dying to Entertain," since 1998, violence on ABC TV has quadrupled (a 309 percent increase—a huge rise, though not quite the "300 times" increase students had mistakenly proclaimed.)

They found that in 1998 the network had about one act of violence per hour (.93). By 2007, it was almost four (3.8) on average. CBS, according to the PTC study, had the highest percentage of deaths during 2005-06, with over 66 percent of violent scenes after 8 p.m. depicting death (www.parents.org). Incidentally, the study points out that, in general, violence in all television shows has shifted to being more central to the story—with more graphic autopsy or torture scenes—than it was over five years ago. It indicates that the 2005-06 season was one of the most violent ever recorded by the PTC.

After each group read its findings aloud, facts discovered by students in the "red group" persuaded the rest of the class, through a show of hands, to agree to limit their television viewing, turning it off completely during the TV-Turnoff Network's TV Turn-off Week—something they were reluctant to do when our television unit began. What this group had discovered, thanks largely to the TV-Turnoff Network's website (http://www.tv-turnoff.org) is that there are more televisions (2.73) in the average home than people (2.55) according to *USA Today*. The average home keeps a television turned on eight hours a day, according to Nielsen (2006). Children who watch six or more hours a day perform worse on reading tests than do those who watch one hour a day or don't play video games, reports the Center for Screentime Awareness (http://www.screentime.org). And by the time they finish high school, children will have spent more hours watching TV than in school.

WHAT DO WE SAY?

I knew students would brainstorm both absurd and frighteningly astute reasons to justify the increase of violence and selfishness on television. My aim was to get these young philosopher-scientists in the habit of asking "why" about their world instead of merely consuming it—of making educated hypotheses, then requiring multiple sources of supporting evidence.

During the group discussion, I learned that they were most troubled by the Senate report statement that television was teaching them to "like killing." The Senate report also claimed that 10 percent of crimes committed are caused by violence seen on television. The study, though predating ours, related the violence they saw on television directly to their present world.

I asked students if they had noticed an increase in violence in their world with the increase in television violence. Jacobo McCarthy and several others fiercely nodded: "Three years ago, I'd only see one or two kids in trouble in the office now and then; now there's up to six or seven," Jacobo commented. I too have noticed an increase in behavior problems at the school since 2001, despite better leadership and more effective intervention. However, increasing poverty and less spending on social services leading to a rise in domestic or neighbor-

> **"WHAT'S SCARY IS KIDS SPEND MORE TIME SEEING TV THAN BEING WITH THEIR DAD.... MAYBE THE PRESIDENT USED TO WATCH MORE TV THAN BEING WITH HIS DAD."**

hood violence could be as equally valid contributors.

"What do you think the reason is behind the increase in television violence?" I asked.

"For brainwashing. TV advertises or sells violence. It influences us to vote for a president who uses war to solve problems," Flynn said.

"I suspect the increase in television violence has something to do with the war on terror," English-learner Andres Ventura emulated his classmate Sebastian Anderson's elevated vocabulary in his summarizing essay. "By scaring kids and parents and pushing violence, people are more likely to vote for war. The TV makes you dumb because if you see a lot, it makes you forget things. It makes parents forget how things were when they were kids."

One of the most shocking facts my students found was that according to the TV-Turnoff Network's Real Vision project, parents spend only 38.5 minutes a day with their children in meaningful conversation. And more than half of 4- to 6-year olds (54 percent) would rather watch TV than spend time with their parents.

This finding inspired Alejandro González's conclusion: "I think George Bush wants to make people more scared. We know George Bush likes war. And...TV makes you like more war. What's scary is kids spend more time seeing TV than being with their dad. Since our study, I turn off the TV more and go play with my dad. Maybe the president used to watch more TV than being with his dad."

"And if Bush isn't responsible? Why would television stations or their advertisers want us to like war?" I asked after reading Alejandro's essay aloud.

"To make money, to sell things and make rich people richer like the people selling guns," Ceilidh said.

"To steal stuff from other countries to make our own country the richest!" Jacobo asserted.

What impact did the students think this increase in television violence and selfishness was having on the world around them?

"TV makes people want violence by making it seem cool," Ceilidh said.

Sebastian added, "Then they want to be part of the army. It's a cycle. TV affects the world, then the world affects the TV, which affects world violence. It's a 'chain reaction of evil,'" Sebastian said, borrowing from a Martin Luther King, Jr. quote I had them memorize for Dr. King's birthday.

"Yeah, TV leads to more fighting. Fighting leads to war," added Jacobo. He evoked Dr. King to finish his thought: "'Hate begetting hate. Wars producing more wars ...' We need to stop or 'we shall all be plunged into the dark abyss of annihilation.'"

It was a peak teaching moment. Students were assimilating valuable things they had learned earlier in the year to shape their thinking about the world. While some of the conclusions tended toward hyperbole, I can't argue with the soundness of my students' hypothesis that television selfishness and violence are part of a propaganda campaign to foment war and enrich certain sectors. But more importantly, my students are learning to think for themselves, to question the sources of their information.

One of my former students, Daniel Hernandez-Deras, once commented that "watching television replaces your imagination with television thinking and there's not much space left after that." Now my current students had begun to turn off the televisions in their own brains and turn on their imagination and curiosity. At last, they had begun to internalize the insight contained in Maeve's essay: "If you watch too much TV, you lose the kid that is inside you," wherein lies our higher inner wisdom. ∎

Margot Pepper (www.margotpepper.com) teaches 2nd grade in a two-way Spanish immersion program at Rosa Parks Elementary School in Berkeley, Calif. Her memoir, Through the Wall: A Year in Havana, *was a top nomination for the 2006 American Book Award.*

Standing Up to Military Recruiters

Story of the Los Angeles Coalition Against Militarism in our Schools

ARLENE INOUYE
RETHINKING SCHOOLS (Spring 2006)

After 20 years of working in the nonprofit sector, I reentered the Los Angeles school district in 1997. I worked as a speech and language specialist in the district and at Theodore Roosevelt High School in East Los Angeles, the same school my mother attended at the onset of World War II.

A lot has changed since my mother attended Roosevelt. Back then, it was a racially diverse school. Now, Roosevelt is the largest school in Los Angeles Unified. Its more than 5,000 students, 95 percent Latina/o and Chicana/o, are on a multitrack, year-round system.

I soon found out that a lot more than the ethnic population of the school had shifted through the years. Uniformed military recruiters roamed the high school campus, freely talking to students. I looked to see if anyone else saw this, and quickly got the sense it was considered normal. I tried to edge my way up close enough to hear what they were saying. The students seemed intrigued, and recruiters were promising money for college and bonus money. I felt helpless and wasn't informed enough to know what to say or do.

> **MILITARY RECRUITERS FLOODED CAMPUSES, RIDING IN HUMVEES THAT BLARED HIP-HOP MUSIC WITH "YO SOY EL ARMY" STICKERS AND FREE T-SHIRTS.**

Eventually, I became a founder of the Coalition Against Militarism in our Schools (CAMS), a grassroots organization of teachers, students, parents, and veterans in the Los Angeles area. CAMS began before the Iraq war as an effort to inform and educate students and the community about the military recruitment that entices our young.

"YO SOY EL ARMY"

After Sept. 11, I joined millions of people in global protest and concern as the Bush administration rushed to war. Military recruiters flooded campuses, riding in humvees that blared hip-hop music with "Yo Soy El Army" stickers and free T-shirts, or in Army vans with pull-up bars. I felt it was my moral duty and responsibility to do everything I could to stop the war and the military recruitment of youth. I knew that it would be schools like mine that would supply soldiers to the military. This troubled me—as a parent who could only imagine losing a child to war, as a teacher who cared about the young lives I see each day, and as a peace and justice activist who believes that war is not the answer and our young should not be cannon fodder.

I began noticing visual manifestations of militarism everywhere from preschool centers to adult education schools, with the most pervasive being at the high schools. I saw National Guard calendars on the walls of the counseling offices, "Go Army" lanyards holding the faculty bathroom key, large cut-out military figures in the hallway, Junior Reserve Officer Training Corps (JROTC) displays with pictures and trophies, and even a Marine Corps insignia on a preschool dedication photo in the school office!

I wondered how this could be justified when the school district had a board policy called "Educating for Diversity" with strategies to create peaceful school climates, teach conflict resolution, promote critical thinking and problem solving, and foster positive human relations through dialogue and nonviolence. I asked teachers and staff what they thought about the military marketing in the schools and began to write articles in the union newsletter about it.

Roosevelt had a reputation as the No. 1 Marine recruiting school in the nation. Military recruiters swarmed the campus and approached the students who seemed the most vulnerable and receptive to the pitch. Some students told me they received telephone calls every week. Military recruiters made unannounced home visits, followed them around campus, and invited them to lunch. Sometimes recruiters played on students' emotions, telling youngsters that they would never make it in college, but they would make their families proud by enlisting.

The climate at Roosevelt changed dramatically in 2003 after an administrator drafted a school policy to set restrictions for military recruiter visits. It surprised the entire school community. She believed there needed to be reasonable restrictions to comply with the No Child Left Behind Act Section 9528 that gives military recruiters the same access as career and college representatives. She acknowledged the fact that military recruiters always had greater access at Roosevelt than career or college recruiters, and their presence did not support academic achievement targets. This school policy passed the school leadership council. It made Roosevelt the only high school out of 60 in the district with an explicit policy restricting military recruiter visits. Military recruiters could no longer approach individual students or make classroom presentations, and could only table at prearranged set times, quarterly or less.

NATIONAL AND LOCAL CONNECTIONS

In June 2003 I attended the first national counter recruitment conference in Philadelphia. It was just what I needed: a national network of activists that provided support and mentoring. (Later, in 2005, we formed the National Network Opposed to the Militarism of Youth, www.youthandthemilitary.org.)

I had high expectations that others would join the counter-recruitment effort in Los Angeles. I announced a meeting in central LA, and told everyone I could reach in the peace and justice community. I went to peace and justice events with flyers and passed out brochures about myths of the military, but in the beginning there were only a handful of people. A breakthrough came when some members of the Human Rights Committee of United Teachers Los Angeles (UTLA) became interested. I had never been active in the teachers' union, feeling that student concerns along with social justice issues were often lost in the fight for teacher rights. But times were different, and now there was a progressive movement in UTLA that joined with other labor unions to form Labor Against the War. The Human Rights Committee designed a T-shirt, "A War Budget Leaves Every Child Behind," and enthusiastically supported a teach-in to begin a dialogue about the war and its impact on our schools and students.

This alliance was significant because we had networking contacts with the 44,000 teacher union members in the district, media contacts, and more clout when we made presentations to the school board. We advertised the teach-in in the union newsletter and distributed hundreds of flyers, which brought in a hundred teachers, students, parents and community members. This marked the beginning of a widespread teacher's network covering all areas of the city and brought us visibility, which soon included a website (www.militaryfreeschools.org), an organizational brochure in English and Spanish, and a phone number.

After a few months, we decided we needed to organize a large citywide event to create a broader network of people to focus on stopping militarism in schools. We planned an all-day conference for February 2004 at an inner-city school, aiming to share the strategies, resources, and experiences of students, education leaders, and peace and justice activists. We settled on a name, Coalition Against Militarism in Our Schools, continued our outreach to the schools and community, and developed a fundraising plan.

We also set out to inform members of the LA Board of Education about the military recruitment abuses occurring at many schools. Students, teachers, parents and community members testified about their experiences. Parents spoke in Spanish with an interpreter and told of unwanted phone calls by recruiters and the involuntary placement of their children into the military program, JROTC, and their difficulty in getting them out. A teacher and community representative from another inner-city school reported how recruiters verbally abused students who passed out antiwar literature. Students testified that no one told them that the ASVAB (Armed Services Vocational Aptitude Battery) was a military exam and a primary source for the Pentagon database. Another student described how a military recruiter offered him a ride home but wouldn't let him out of the car until he gave his contact information.

Later, the board president told me that board members didn't know what was going on in the local schools until we informed them. The board formed a District Advisory Military Recruitment Committee, which gave us direct access to district staff and information. We had quarterly meetings where we raised questions and requested clarification about processes and policies with school officials and military personnel. At times the process was slow and frustrating, especially when district officials dodged our requests, but we gained tangible results from this collaboration. The most significant of those results was a districtwide policy that spells out limits on military recruiter access to students. For the first time the nation's second largest school district had written parameters for military recruitment.

ALTERNATIVES TO THE MILITARY

Our goal in CAMS includes a mission beyond the immediate issue of militarism in the schools. We want to transform the school climate and promote peaceful alternatives, social justice, and hope for youth. We want students to have the opportunity to explore their dreams and passions and to know that they can choose viable careers and go to college without joining the military. We developed a booklet called "Great Jobs, Careers, Futures" and a separate higher education brochure.

One strategy we pursued was our Operation Opt Out Campaign, which focused on the insufficient ways that the LAUSD was complying with the opt-out clause in NCLB. We presented our concerns regarding the notification process to the board of education: short timeline,

---

> **LA Unified School District**
> **Military Recruitment Policy**
>
> - **No student is required by the school to meet with or speak to a recruiter.**
>
> - **No student will be required to take the Armed Services Vocational Aptitude Battery (ASVAB) test.**
>
> - **Participation in JROTC is voluntary and students will not be forced to take JROTC class in lieu of regular physical education class.**
>
> - **Students age 17 and older will be allowed to opt out of sending personal information to military recruiters without parental approval.**
>
> - **The military will not be allowed to bring military equipment or vehicles to campus unless the district has approved it.**
>
> - **The military cannot suggest students drop out of high school and pursue a GED as a means of recruiting.**
>
> **See www.militaryfreeschools.org for the entire policy.**

---

confusing information, failure to communicate rights to students. And we developed our own plan for getting the word out through student groups, flyers to teacher union representatives, and at peace and justice community events. CAMS developed and distributed thousands of fact sheets with the opt-out form on the back in English and Spanish.

This campaign triggered an outpouring of student organizing. Students set up tables and crafted large opt-out signs to get the information out to their peers. They passed out flyers and counter recruitment literature, and made multimedia presentations. At one school an administrator refused to publicize the opt-out information through a public announcement. When students learned about this resistance from teachers, many of them (including the uniformed football team) stormed the principal's office.

When the opt-out returns were announced, we were ecstatic. We had reached our goal of 5,000 more students than the previous year—a total of 11,350 students or 18 percent of 63,000 juniors and seniors in LAUSD). Roosevelt High School nearly tripled its number of students opting out from 200 to 600. In 2005, the opt-out numbers increased to 24 percent, more than 15,000 students.

But more important than the numbers were the experiences that came out of this campaign. One student, Michelle Villegas, initiated passing out counter-recruitment flyers with her MEChA (Movimiento Estudiantil

> **TODAY, STUDENTS FROM MEChA AND OTHER ORGANIZATIONS WEAR HANDMADE T-SHIRTS WITH SAYINGS LIKE "BOOKS NOT BOMBS" AND "STUDENTS NOT SOLDIERS."**

Chicano de Aztlan). The principal stopped her, saying that she needed administrator approval. Her mother searched the Internet for ways to support Michelle and found CAMS. Mrs. Villegas wrote to us and asked for help. I received her email, wrote a response, and copied it to the ACLU. After a meeting with the district lawyer, the administration changed its position and allowed students to distribute flyers wherever they wanted. But it didn't stop there. This incident energized Michelle and her mother to join CAMS and take the leadership at their high school.

ADOPT-A-SCHOOL PROJECT

We realized that as more people became interested in helping us, we needed to provide clear and specific steps on what to do. Some community members and veterans who did not have children in schools wanted to help, but didn't know how to start. We envisioned the neighborhood schools as centers of activism where the broader community could participate. So we developed the CAMS Adopt-a-School Project and Tool Kit to show step-by-step process how anyone can help demilitarize schools and present alternatives.

Today when you visit Roosevelt High School in East Los Angeles, you will find a very different school climate. Military recruiters claim "Roosevelt has kicked us out" and they are no longer interested in coming to campus. Instead, students from MEChA and other organizations wear handmade T-shirts with sayings like "Books not Bombs" and "Students not Soldiers," and pass out counter-recruitment fliers and college informational brochures. They are all a testament to the organizing work of many that started with a few.

CAMS has grown beyond my wildest expectations. It has taught me about organizing and the power of working together. But the greatest reward comes in those quiet moments when a student will say, "I was going to join the military, but what you've shown me has changed my mind. Everyone needs to know about this." ▪

Arlene Inouye (arlene@militaryfreeschools.org) works as a speech and language specialist in East Los Angeles. She is a founder of the Coalition Against Militarism in Our Schools (www.militaryfreeschools.org), which was awarded a 2006 Human Rights Award from the California Teachers Association.

Resources

Committee Opposed to Militarism and the Draft (COMD) www.comdsd.org

American Friends Service Committee (AFSC) www.afsc.org

Guerrero Azteca (Fernando Suarez del Solar) www.guerreroazteca.org

War Resisters League www.warresisters.org

Project Youth and Nonmilitary Options www.projectyano.org

GI Rights Hotline www.girightshotline.org ▪ 877-447-4487

Arlington West film www.arlingtonwestfilm.com

Veterans For Peace www.veteransforpeace.org

Iraq Veterans Against the War www.ivaw.net

Addicted to War www.addictedtowar.com

Gold Star Families for Peace www.gsfp.org

Soldiers Speak Out www.empowermentproject.org.

MICHAEL DUFFY

Draft Resolution to End Military Recruitment Abuse

RETHINKING SCHOOLS (Fall 2005)

Whereas: No Child Left Behind regulations (Section 9528) require that public secondary schools "shall provide military recruiters the same access to secondary school students as is provided generally to post secondary educational institutions or to prospective employers of those students;" and

Whereas: Portland secondary teachers, counselors, parents, and students report that military recruiters have pursued students aggressively, including: arriving at high schools without invitation, approaching students with no supervision by school authorities, contacting students by phone and email even when requested not to do so by parents and students themselves, visiting students' homes, buying students gifts, lying to and misleading students about military life and military regulations (including making promises that recruits will not be sent to Iraq), manipulating or casting aspersions upon students' post-high school hopes, approaching students in their classes, participating in curricular and extracurricular activities at school (even bringing weapons on campus); and

Whereas: Military access is disturbingly uneven from one Portland high school to another and tends to be more intense in schools serving predominantly low- or middle-income neighborhoods; and

Whereas: It is the responsibility of Portland Public Schools to promote the welfare of students while at school and at school events, and to provide students with complete and accurate information about the choices they will confront upon graduation from high school; therefore:

As is true throughout much of the United States, in Portland, Ore., military recruiters lie to and mislead high school students. They show up uninvited on campus. They call students at home. They ask personal questions about students' future plans and then assure them that the best way these can be realized is by first joining the military.

Want to go to college? Join the military. Want to be a musician? Join the military. Want to kickbox? Join the military. Not surprisingly, recruiters frequent schools serving working class and low-income communities. This resolution was drafted by a group of teachers and activists who decided that without a districtwide policy, recruitment abuses were sure to continue or even increase. They hope to build community support for the resolution and to have it introduced at a future school board meeting.

Be it resolved that pursuant to the NCLB Act, Portland Public School officials will provide military recruiters no greater access to students than that provided to post secondary educational institutions or prospective employers, and will provide student information to U.S. military authorities only after obtaining permission to do so in writing by an individual student, or by a parent or guardian of the student; and

Be it further resolved that any vendors with access to student information through legitimate business dealings with a school and/or a school's students may not give, lend, or sell this information to the military or risk being banned from doing business with Portland Public Schools; and

Be it further resolved that in accordance with Section 9528 of No Child Left Behind, military recruiters shall be granted no special access to students; specifically, recruiters: 1) must secure prior permission before coming onto a high school campus; 2) may engage in recruitment activities no more than once per year; 3) may not participate in any extra-curricular activities, including but not limited to field day events, graduation ceremonies, school assemblies, or sporting events; 4) may not bring weapons, Humvees, or other military equipment onto a high school campus for any purpose whatsoever; 5) may meet with students only by appointment and only in a designated counseling or career center; and 6) may not participate in the design or teaching of any course curriculum; and

Be it further resolved that Portland Public Schools students, staff, and parents shall be informed at least two weeks prior to military recruiters coming on campus—publicized in the same manner as for other institutional recruiters; and

Be it further resolved that if a military recruiter is found to have lied to a student, he or she shall be permanently banned from Portland Public Schools; and

Be it finally resolved that recruiters shall not be allowed on the campus of any Portland elementary or middle school.

Regaining My Humanity

Acting upon my principles became incompatible with my role in the military, and I decided that I could not return to Iraq

CAMILO MEJIA
RETHINKING SCHOOLS (Fall 2005)

I was deployed to Iraq in April 2003 and returned home for a two-week leave in October. Going home gave me the opportunity to put my thoughts in order and to listen to what my conscience had to say.

People would ask me about my war experiences and answering them took me back to all the horrors—the firefights, the ambushes, the time I saw a young Iraqi dragged by his shoulders through a pool of his own blood, or the time I saw an innocent man decapitated by our machine gun fire. Or the time I saw a soldier broken down inside because he killed a child, or the time I saw an old man on his knees, crying with his arms raised to the sky, perhaps asking God why we had taken the lifeless body of his son. I thought of the suffering of a people whose country was in ruins and who were further humiliated by the raids, patrols, and curfews of an occupying army.

And I realized that none of the reasons we were told about why we were in Iraq turned out to be true. There were no weapons of mass destruction. There was no link between Saddam Hussein and al Qaeda. We weren't helping the Iraqi people and the Iraqi people didn't want us there. We weren't preventing terrorism or making Americans safer. I couldn't find a single good reason for having been there, for having shot at people and been shot at.

Coming home gave me the clarity to see the line between military duty and moral obligation. I realized that I was part of a war that I believed was immoral and criminal, a war of aggression, a war of imperial domination. I realized that acting upon my principles became incompatible with my role in the military, and I decided that I could not return to Iraq.

By putting my weapon down, I chose to reassert myself as a human being. I have not deserted the military or been disloyal to the men and women of the military. I have not been disloyal to a country. I have only been loyal to my principles.

When I turned myself in, with all my fears and doubts, I did it not only for myself. I did it for the people of Iraq, even for those who fired upon me—they were just on the other side of a battleground where war itself was the only enemy. I did it for the Iraqi children, who are victims of mines and depleted uranium. I did it for the thousands of unknown civilians killed in war. My time in prison is a small price compared to the price Iraqis and Americans have paid with their

Carlos Mejia served as a U.S. infantryman from 1995 until 1998, and then continued his contract as a reservist in the Florida National Guard. In March 2004, having served seven months in the Middle East—including five months of combat in Iraq—he filed for discharge as a conscientious objector. He had concluded that the war against and occupation of Iraq was "illegal and immoral" and he refused to fight.

In May 2004, he was sentenced by a special court-martial to the maximum penalty of one year in prison for desertion. This statement comes from Mejia's application for conscientious objection and his prison writings. He was released from the Army prison at Fort Sill, Okla., in 2005.

TO THOSE WHO HAVE CALLED ME A HERO, I SAY THAT I DON'T BELIEVE IN HEROES, BUT I BELIEVE THAT ORDINARY PEOPLE CAN DO EXTRAORDINARY THINGS.

lives. Mine is a small price compared to the price humanity has paid for war.

Many have called me a coward. Others have called me a hero. I believe I can be found somewhere in the middle. To those who have called me a hero, I say that I don't believe in heroes, but I believe that ordinary people can do extraordinary things.

To those who have called me a coward I say that they are wrong, and that without knowing it, they are also right. They are wrong when they think that I left the war for fear of being killed. I admit that fear was there, but there was also the fear of killing innocent people, the fear of putting myself in a position where to survive means to kill. There was the fear of losing my soul in the process of saving my body, the fear of losing myself—to my daughter, to the people who love me, to the man I used to be, the man I wanted to be. I was afraid of waking up one morning to realize my humanity had abandoned me.

I say without any pride that I did my job as a soldier. I commanded an infantry squad in combat and we never failed to accomplish our mission. But those who called me a coward, without knowing it, are also right. I was a coward not for leaving the war, but for having been a part of it in the first place. Refusing and resisting this war was my moral duty, a moral duty that called me to take a principled action. I failed to fulfill my moral duty as a human being and instead I chose to fulfill my duty as a soldier. All because I was afraid. I was terrified, I did not want to stand up to the government and the Army, I was afraid of punishment and humiliation. I went to war because at the moment I was a coward, and for that I apologize to my soldiers for not being the type of leader I should have been.

I also apologize to the Iraqi people. To them I say I am sorry for the curfews, for the raids, for the killings. May they find it in their hearts to forgive me.

One of the reasons I did not refuse the war from the beginning was that I was afraid of losing my freedom. Today, as I sit behind bars I realize that there are many types of freedom, and that in spite of my confinement I remain free in many important ways. What good is freedom if we are afraid to follow our conscience? What good is freedom if we are not able to live with our own actions? I am confined to a prison but I feel, today more than ever, connected to all humanity. Behind these bars I sit a free man because I listened to a higher power, the voice of my conscience.

To those who are still quiet, to those who continue to betray their conscience, to those who are not calling evil more clearly by its name, to those of us who are still not doing enough to refuse and resist, I say "come forward." I say "free your minds." Let us, collectively, free our minds, soften our hearts, comfort the wounded, put down our weapons, and reassert ourselves as human beings by putting an end to war. ▪

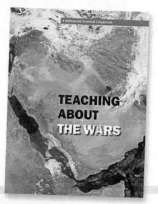

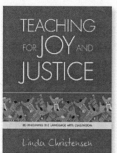

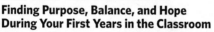

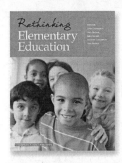

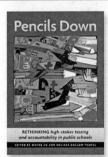

**If you liked *Teaching About the Wars*,
then *Rethinking Schools* magazine is for you!**
Take advantage of this special discount coupon to receive
the country's leading social justice education magazine.

....

INTRODUCTORY OFFER! *Subscribe today and save!*

□ Two years (8 issues) for $22.95 *(Save $24.65 off the cover price!)*
□ One year (4 issues) for $14.95 *(Save $8.85 off the cover price!)*
□ Print version *or* □ Digital version.

□ Please send me a free catalog of all your materials.
□ Bill me. □ Enclosed is my check payable to *Rethinking Schools*.

*See our website for combined digital/print subscription options.
Add $10 per year for all international print subscriptions.*

**"A teacher's close friend
—insightful, intelligent,
and
compassionate."**
*– Michele Forman,
Teacher of the Year*

Name _____

Organization _____

Address _____

City/State/Zip _____

Phone _____

Email _____

RETHINKINGSCHOOLS
PO Box 2222, Williston, VT 05495 • toll-free: 800-669-4192 • fax: 802-864-7626

2BTeAb

....

INTRODUCTORY OFFER! *Subscribe today and save!*

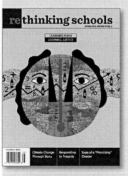

□ Two years (8 issues) for $22.95 *(Save $24.65 off the cover price!)*
□ One year (4 issues) for $14.95 *(Save $8.85 off the cover price!)*
□ Print version *or* □ Digital version.

□ Please send me a free catalog of all your materials.
□ Bill me. □ Enclosed is my check payable to *Rethinking Schools*.

*See our website for combined digital/print subscription options.
Add $10 per year for all international print subscriptions.*

**"Absolutely the best,
most important   edu-
cation publication   in
the country."**
– Jonathan Kozol

Name _____

Organization _____

Address _____

City/State/Zip _____

Phone _____

Email _____

RETHINKINGSCHOOLS
PO Box 2222, Williston, VT 05495 • toll-free: 800-669-4192 • fax: 802-864-7626

2BTeAb